Butter

a celebration

Olivia Potts

Butter

a celebration

Olivia Potts

For Elwood, of course

First published in 2022 by Headline Home,
an imprint of Headline Publishing Group
Carmelite House
50 Victoria Embankment
London EC4Y 0DZ
www.headline.co.uk

An Hachette UK Company
www.hachette.co.uk

ISBN 978 1 4722 8464 8
eISBN 978 1 4722 8466 2

A CIP catalogue record for this book is available from the British Library.

Printed and bound in Italy.

10 9 8 7 6 5 4 3 2 1

Headline's policy is to use papers that are natural, renewable and recyclable
products and made from wood grown in well-managed forests and other controlled
sources. The logging and manufacturing processes are expected to conform to the
environmental regulations of the country of origin.

Publisher: Lindsey Evans
Project Editors: Dan Hurst and Kate Miles
Assistant Editor: Kathryn Allen
Designer: Matt Cox at Newman+Eastwood
Photographer: Matt Russell
Food and Prop Stylist: Emma Lahaye
Copy Editor: Annie Lee
Proofreader: Anne Sheasby
Indexer: Caroline Wilding
Senior Production Controller: Tina Paul

Ovens should be preheated to the specific temperature – if using a fan-assisted
oven, follow manufacturer's instructions for adjusting the time and the temperature.
Pepper should be freshly ground black pepper unless otherwise stated.

(i.e. where yeast is involved), or where the recipe combines something salty directly with the butter (like the Marmite butter, or the anchovy butter), but with the exception of that handful of recipes, you can make any recipe in this book with salted or unsalted butter – just get into the habit of tasting the dish as you go, checking for balance and seasoning accordingly.

And it's really important to adjust the seasoning, even (especially!) in sweet dishes, to balance the competing flavours, and stop it becoming one note. If you're nervous about this, salted butter can go a long way to doing the work for you. The difference between a good cookie and a great cookie is usually salt.

Rapidly diminishing returns

I've resisted the occasional urge to scale down the butter in the recipes. It might sound silly to say that that's something that has been tempting, but now and again, I'd find myself raising an eyebrow at the amount of butter in a particular recipe. And I worried that if I didn't adjust down that amount of butter, it might be off-putting. I imagined a conversation: 'Good GOD, do you know how much butter goes into a baklava?! I can never have one again!' It makes me miserable just to think about it. Butter is about taste and pleasure, and to sacrifice butter would be to sacrifice both of those.

The thing is, baklava does have a lot of butter in it. That's why it's so maddeningly delicious. Do you know what makes mashed potatoes great? Butter. Why does restaurant food taste so damn good? Butter. Butter is what makes puff pastry and croissant dough and brioche so incredible. It would be ridiculous for me to underplay the role butter plays in them. Scaling down the butter diminishes the dish, and that goes against everything I care about. So I promised myself there would be no diminishing, no minimising. Instead, my imaginary conversation goes like this: 'That's how much butter goes into a baklava? That's how they make it so good! Now I can make it myself.'

Sustainable dairy farming

While butter is the only animal fat which can be produced without requiring the slaughter of an animal, it would be wrong in a book about butter to pretend that the dairy industry is unproblematic. Ethically and ecologically there are real issues: the premature removal of calves from their mother, the killing of dairy bull calves, the rampant use of antibiotics, crowded living conditions for the herds, and poor welfare and health of animals. Dairy farmers are paid disgracefully poorly, and supermarkets exacerbate the problem by dropping the price of dairy products to an unsustainable level. This has led to intensive farming, and the advent of mega-dairies and factory farming.

However, there are many dairy farms doing very good work, and if you're going to consume dairy products, the best thing you can do is support them: buy direct from dairies and producers, and be prepared to pay more for butter and cream that comes from dairies with high welfare standards. There are farms that are seeking more sustainable means of production: dairies which keep calves with their mothers until naturally weaned, dairies that enable free-grazing for cattle. Small dairies can be hugely beneficial for biodiversity, and mitigate the impact of increased emissions by regenerating the soil they use.

If you eat meat, make a point of seeking out ex-dairy cows when you buy beef. British farmers have started following the example of Basque farmers: after a lifetime of milking, the dairy cows (which otherwise wouldn't be used for meat) are retired on to pastureland. The meat that is then produced is intensely flavoured, with beautiful marbling.

Blowing hot and cold

The temperature of the butter you use for a recipe that majors in butter is integral. It makes the difference between the most beautiful, rippling silk of a buttercream that you have ever seen, easy to use and melting as it hits the tongue, and buttercream that looks like soup, or tastes greasy and crumbly. It's the difference between perfectly laminated, easy to handle pastry, and one where the layers disappear and you end up covered in butter. It is near impossible to properly cream cold butter for a cake. Equally, don't even try grating butter for pastry that hasn't spent at least a short spell in the freezer.

So, when I say cold butter I mean butter that has been in the fridge at least overnight. When I say 'soft' or 'softened' butter, I mean butter that has been at room temperature for at least 12 hours. When I say 'very soft' butter, I mean you should be able to swipe a finger through it without resistance. The French call this softness of butter 'beurre pomade', because it has the texture of hair wax.

Don't substitute melted butter if you forget to leave your butter out: when butter melts, its natural emulsion is broken, so it behaves differently. Instead, if you forget to soften the butter in time, exerting force on it will do a similar job. The crystals in butter will only break apart and melt at 35°C, but you can manually separate them by scraping them (as with a butter knife), bashing them between two sheets of baking paper with a rolling pin, or, in dire straits, putting the butter into a food processor.

Some practicalities: notes on measurements, ingredients, temperatures and machines

Oven temperatures

All the recipes here have been developed and tested in fan ovens. Ovens are notoriously temperamental: they have hot spots and cool spots. It's all very well me superciliously telling you to get an oven thermometer to sense check, or even calibrate, your oven thermostat, but that's no good if you remember my incredible wisdom halfway through baking a batch of scones. And if I'm honest, I have an oven thermometer, and I check it as often as I defrost my freezer.

So I've tried to make sure that the recipes include cues that will tell you when dishes are ready. A sponge cake is a good example: when it's ready, it won't smell at all eggy, it will have slightly pulled away from the sides of the tin; if you put your ear close to it, you shouldn't hear any hissing or 'singing', and if you press its middle gently with a fingertip, it should spring back. Be guided by the sensory descriptions over and above the timings I give.

Ingredients

All recipe writers urge you to use the best quality ingredients you can afford, and of course that's true and important: not only will your food taste better if you're using high quality produce, but when you're using meat, fish or dairy products, this is particularly important from a sustainability point of view. You will be doing the farmer, the animal, and the world a favour.

Eggs

Don't feel like you have to use large eggs. It's become normal for recipes to stipulate large eggs, but recently, egg producers have campaigned for food writers to change their thinking. Demanding large eggs creates, well, a demand for large eggs. And the eggs that don't meet that grade can't be sold. This is an unforgivable and unnecessary waste. The difference between egg sizes isn't enough to make or break any of the recipes in this book.

Pâtisserie loves an egg yolk, but can therefore generate a lot of unused egg whites. In a domestic kitchen particularly, this seems silly. So, if you find yourself overloaded with egg whites, please turn straight to page 256 for brilliant, brown butter and hazelnut honey friands, or to pages 216 and 218 for Swiss meringue and Italian buttercreams, all of which use egg whites in spades. Egg whites also keep well in the fridge and freezer, as does meringue-based buttercream – just let it come back to room temperature, and give it a good whip before using.

Butter

For the recipes which use lamination (puff pastry, croissant dough and brioche feuilletée) you need butter with a minimum fat percentage of 82%. Most British butters will meet this, or be only marginally lower, but if you're cooking in a different country, do check. A lower fat percentage means a higher water percentage, and this presents problems when the pastry cooks.

Chilling

You're going to find a lot of 'leave to chill' instructions in this book. Butter is a tricksy little bugger, and your life will be immeasurably easier if you're able to give the components time to chill when directed. Your pastry will be easier to roll, your tart cases won't shrink, your custard will be thick and luscious. But equally, I'll let you know when overnight chilling is an ideal rather than a necessity.

Yeast

I prefer to use dried, instant (fast action/easy blend) yeast: it has a very long shelf-life, produces consistent results, and doesn't need any faffing with before I can use it. But other bakers have different preferences, and sometimes we just can't get our hands on exactly what we need. So, as a rule of thumb, you can double the amount of instant yeast to give you the correct amount for active dried yeast, or quadruple it to get the right amount of fresh yeast. Both active dried yeast and fresh yeast will need to be activated before you start using them: place them in a container with a teaspoon of sugar and a small amount of warm water or milk – however much liquid you use to bloom your yeast, remove that from the total amount of liquid in your recipe. And you want it to be just above body temperature, so as not to kill off the yeast.

Horse power

It is easier to make many of the more complicated pastry recipes using a stand mixer, and for the purposes of the recipes, this will be my first suggestion. It it is possible to make them – even brioche, croissant and buttercream – by hand without a stand mixer, but it's hard: it takes more time, and more elbow grease.

20 Homemade butter

22 Smoked butter

24 Cultured butter

26 Compound butters

42 Niter Kibbeh (Ethiopian spiced butter)

43 Smen

CHAPTER 1
BUTTER

Butter

Butter has the ability to change the way you cook and the way you eat. It will bring richness and silkiness, lightness and flakiness to all manner of dishes. For the other chapters in this book, butter is a building block; here it is the end product, the goal, the reward. And there are all sorts of ways to change the experience of eating that butter.

Making and handling butter is the intersection of science and magic: the breaking down of one emulsion – cream – through pure agitation to allow another emulsion – butter – to form. It feels like modern kitchen alchemy. And it's one of those rare bits of culinary transformation, like making honeycomb or baking bread, that doesn't require lots of ingredients or fancy equipment. Butter can be made with just a pint of cream, a bowl and a whisk.

The way we made and ate butter used to be a mere practicality: butter itself was a method for preserving the cream which wasn't going to be used by the end of the day. Originally, all butter used to be cultured – not so much through design, as by the sheer fact that before refrigeration, the cream would be left out in pails and, in the ambient temperature, would just slightly ferment; and salting butter was born out of necessity too, a way of extending its life by deterring the bacteria which causes butter to spoil.

Many of the necessities of old-fashioned butter making have seen a resurgence because these are now things that we prize in our butter: small-batch, hand-made, cultured butter. With centrifugal cream separators and refrigeration, there is no *need* for these ways of making butter any more, but it is the best way of showing off the finest ingredients, and the creativity of the producer. And these are also methods of making butter that you can use easily at home which will be head and shoulders above any supermarket branded butter you've bought.

Think of cultured butter as the butter equivalent of sourdough: it needs a small helping hand from pre-existing bacteria in the form of a fermented starter (a spoonful of crème fraîche will do the job), and then given time to get to know that bacteria at room temperature. Similarly to sourdough, the result is (once churned) something that is recognisably butter, but more interesting, more delicious: slightly acidic, funky, cheesey, complicated. You can use cultured butter wherever you'd use uncultured butter (it just might talk to you about Wagner or the new Hilary Mantel). I make cultured butter to spread thickly on good bread or hot toast – but I also use it in recipes where that butter can shine: in shortbreads, or on a tumble of simply steamed green veg. It's also great for puff pastry and viennoiserie, as it has a slightly higher fat content than uncultured butter.

Making your own butter is just the beginning: once you've done it, you can play around with bringing different flavours and qualities to that butter.

Butter's ability to carry flavour is unparalleled, which means compound butters – where ingredients have been bashed into the butter – are brilliant ways of enjoying classic, clever and unusual flavour combinations, whether you're using them to flavour your cooking, or smearing them on to bread. There are few things that bring me greater joy in the kitchen than having a handful of baking paper sausages in my fridge, with snub bottoms and little twisted ends, filled with flavoured butters – from tarragon and vinegar that make the butter taste like béarnaise sauce, to a tablespoon of Marmite turning the butter tawny. Frosty, boozy brandy butter, spiced with a little nutmeg, melting on to a thick slab of Christmas pudding, or chipotle and coriander rippling red and green through the yellow butter, like an edible traffic light.

Burning or browning butter changes its structure but also produces something unique, with an entirely different character to unbrowned butter. What you're doing really when you burn or brown butter is caramelising the milk solids in the butter, and this gives the butter all the good things that go along with caramelisation: a simultaneous sweetness and savouriness, neither of which were there in the raw product, and a smokiness and nuttiness.

But of course, burning butter has been an integral part of cooking, both classical French cooking and worldwide, for many, many years: classical sauces like beurre noisette, used to dress fish, vegetables and meat, require it, as do cakes like madeleines. Around the world, cultures have clarified butter slowly, slowly until the butter turns nut brown, and the milk solids fall away, creating ghee, smen and niter kibbeh, giving the butter indefinite shelf-life and a deep flavour, perfect for cooking with at high temperatures or storing at room temperature in hot countries. As well as these traditional uses, I use it to offset sweetness and bring depth of flavour in sugar-heavy bakes like blondies, to spoon over pasta, and to swirl through mashed potatoes.

Buttermilk – the by-product of butter making – is an invaluable bonus: on those occasions I absent-mindedly go to strain the butter into the sink, and see that beautiful buttermilk falling down the drain, I curse myself. Buttermilk has a myriad of uses: due to its acidity it is as effective as a tenderising marinade on meat as it is a catalyst for alkaline raising agents in cakes, breads and pancakes, so strain the milk into a small bowl, and keep the buttermilk in the fridge for another recipe. Just don't expect it to be like the stuff you buy from the shops: it will be thinner in texture and brighter in flavour. Many cultures drink it in that form, but I like to save it and use it for making perfect fried chicken, ridiculously fluffy pancakes, and the best soda bread you've ever eaten (see page 186).

Once you've churned your own butter, the world is your (buttered, grilled) oyster.

Homemade butter

If you've never made your own butter before, you're in for a treat. It feels more like a science experiment than a recipe, but the end, the result is significantly more satisfying and delicious than a potato clock.

Cream is an emulsion and it will break if sufficiently agitated: when that emulsion breaks, the fat will separate out and clump together. If you've ever over-whisked cream until it becomes slightly grainy, or yellow-tinged, or even buttery tasting, you're 85% of the way there to making proper butter. That yellow is the first sign of butter: cow milk and cream contain beta-carotene, which is in the grass the cows eat. In milk and cream, it is stored within the fat molecules, and the membrane around them disguises the daffodil yellow. As the emulsion breaks, so too do those membranes, and the sunshine-yellow butter spills out.

I tend to make my butter in a food processor, whizzing the cream on top speed until it stiffens, slackens, and eventually turns golden: it's fast, and causes the least mess. For a long time, I used my stand mixer, whisking the cream, until it split – just make sure you cover the gap between the top of the bowl and the head of the mixer, as when the cream separates, the buttermilk will splash all over the place. But I've done it by hand too, and it's extremely doable: you only need a bowl and a whisk, and a little bit of patience and some elbow grease.

For all its methodological simplicity, butter can also be complex, and no two butters are the same. Butter can be rich or acidic, sweet or salty, nutty or grassy, fresh or funky – some manage to be all of the above. Each butter's character is dictated by a combination of the cow, the grass, the soil, the dairy farmer, the butter churner. There is as much a sense of place in a pat of butter, and butter has as much of a claim to terroir, as the finest cheese or wine.

Once the buttermilk and the butter solids have separated (and you'll know when they do: the buttermilk will splosh out of the mix), the butter needs washing. Washing the butter removes any excess buttermilk, which would cause the butter to spoil if left in. If you don't have butter paddles (I don't), or can't be bothered with them (I can't), you can do this by kneading the butter in a little bit of very cold water until the water clouds, then switching in fresh water, and repeating until the water remains clear.

Nowadays, with the invention of refrigeration, salting your butter isn't necessary to preserve it, but, as with anything you're seasoning, it improves the flavour, bringing out the complexities in the butter. Do what you would do with any other dish: season, taste to see if it's sufficiently salty, and add more salt if not. I like to salt butter with good quality flaky salt, so that some of the salt crystals dissolve in the mixture, and some sit glistening in the butter, and pop on your tongue.

Your homemade butter will not have the shelf-life of the stuff you get from the shops, as it lacks preservatives (that's part of the joy of it, of course) – it will keep well in the fridge for a couple of weeks, but shouldn't really be left out more than a few days at room temperature.

Makes: 150g butter

Hands-on time: 15 minutes

Total time: 15 minutes

300ml cold double cream

flaky salt, to taste

1. You can churn butter using a food processor, a stand mixer with a whisk attachment, a hand-held electric whisk, or by hand using a balloon whisk. If you're using a stand mixer, you'll need to cover the gap between the bowl and frame of the mixer with clingfilm to prevent the buttermilk splashing everywhere. Place the cream in a clean, deep bowl, or in the bowl of your machine.

2. Whichever equipment you choose, the key is to beat and agitate the cream as you would if you were whipping it. So whisk or process it until it forms soft peaks, then stiff peaks, then begins to split. As the cream's emulsion breaks, the buttermilk will splash out, and little globules of golden butter ('popcorn butter') will start to appear: continue whisking or processing until the butter clumps together.

3. Holding back the solids, decant the buttermilk into a container and save for other recipes, like fried chicken, pancakes, or soda bread (page 186).

4. To wash the butter, first place it under running cold water: you want to wash away as much of the liquid in the butter as possible, to prevent it spoiling. Now, place the butter in a dry bowl. Fill a small jug with cold water and add a couple of ice cubes. Pour a little of the iced water over the butter, and knead the butter in the bowl: squash it, flatten it, ball it back up again, press it against the sides of the bowl. The water will turn cloudy; pour it off, and add a little more clean iced water. Keep going until the water doesn't cloud when you knead the butter.

5. Pat the butter dry with a little kitchen paper; if there are small beads of water appearing in the butter then you need to remove more buttermilk, so add a little more ice water and knead again.

6. Using a stand mixer or spatula, beat the salt into the butter. Place in a ramekin, or roll into a sausage using a strip of baking paper, and twist the ends to secure.

Smoked butter

Smoked butter is absurdly delicious. Like, once-you've-tasted-it-you'll-dream-about-it good. It does what it says on the tin: the butter is slowly infused with wood smoke. Cold-smoking means that you can bring the delicate flavour of woodsmoke to products that you don't want to cook – smoked salmon, smoked cheese, smoked salt. Butter takes on the smoky flavour brilliantly because, as we saw in the introduction, the fat makes it a great flavour carrier.

You can buy cold smokers for home smoking: small, square metal containers designed like a little maze, which you then place in your kettle barbecue, set smouldering, close the lid, and leave to do their thing. Follow the instructions on your smoker, but my two top tips for cold-smoking after a bunch of failures is to dry out the wood shavings in the oven at a low temperature for 30 minutes before using, and make sure you fill the maze generously with the wood shavings, otherwise it will struggle to stay alight. And don't smoke on a hot day: you need the butter to remain solid for the whole smoking period, and a sunny, summer day will make this trickier.

The longer you smoke, the smokier the flavour of the finished butter. Two hours of cold smoking is about right for my tastes – distinctively smoky but not overwhelming – but try it and see how you like it: you can always pop it in for longer if it's not strong enough for you.

Although there is a cheat: if you don't fancy or have the capacity for cold smoking, you can get a pretty good effect just by swapping the flaked sea salt you'd normally stir through it in favour of smoked salt. Most of the major supermarkets now produce their own brand of smoked salt. If you use the good stuff, it will bring a pretty convincing depth.

Makes: 150g smoked butter

Hands-on time: Less than 5 minutes

Total time: 2 hours

150g butter

1. Using a spatula or stand-mixer, beat your butter to soften it a little. Place your butter in a heatproof container, ideally with a large surface area to help it absorb the smoke.

2. Follow the instructions on your cold smoker. For me, this means drying out my wood shavings in the oven, and setting the smoker up in my kettle barbecue.

3. Smoke for approximately 2 hours, then taste to see if the butter is smoked to your taste – you can always put it back in the smoker for longer, if you want a more pronounced flavour.

Béarnaise butter

Béarnaise sauce (page 59) is hands down my favourite accompaniment to a thick-cut, rare-cooked, rib-eye steak. But it really isn't something that you can make in advance, as it'll split if it cools down. Sometimes I'm happy to stand over a stove just before dinner, but sometimes I want to have three vodka martinis and a bowl of crisps instead. This butter has all the flavours of béarnaise sauce (tarragon, shallot, white wine vinegar), but with the added joy of being made in a matter of moments hours earlier, and sitting in the fridge, pistachio green, just waiting to be sliced and slung on to a really great piece of meat.

75g butter, soft

1 tablespoon finely chopped fresh tarragon

1 small shallot, finely diced

1½ tablespoons white wine vinegar

Whizz together the ingredients in a food processor until smooth; you may need to pause the processor and scrape down the sides a few times. Roll into a sausage using a strip of baking paper, twist the ends to secure, and refrigerate until firm.

Chicken skin butter

Chicken skin butter is perhaps my ideal compound butter: not just because it makes the eyes of those eating it widen in surprise, but because it tastes fantastic. You're going to need the chicken skin and not the meat from the chicken: I have a little Tupperware in my freezer, and every time I buy chicken thighs (the best bit of the skin for this recipe) that aren't being roasted or pan-fried, I sling the skin into this Tupperware so I can make chicken skin butter.

75g chicken skin

¼ teaspoon flaky salt

100g butter, soft

Put the chicken skin pieces in a cold heavy-based frying pan, season them with the salt, and turn the heat on low. Leave the skin to cook slowly, turning the bits of skin every now and again, until the whole thing has given up its fat, and is golden-brown and crisp. This takes about 15 minutes. When cool enough to handle, chop the skin into very small pieces using a sharp knife.

Beat the butter until soft, then sprinkle the chicken skin pieces over the top, and beat until they are evenly distributed throughout the butter. Place in a ramekin, or roll into a sausage using a strip of baking paper, twist the ends to secure, and refrigerate until firm.

Dill, pink peppercorn and sea salt butter

If you're eating smoked salmon on thickly buttered brown bread (the ultimate teatime treat), try bashing chopped dill and crushed pink peppercorns into the butter. A little grated lemon or orange zest is a great addition here.

100g unsalted butter, soft

½ teaspoon flaky salt

¼ teaspoon pink peppercorns, bashed

½ teaspoon finely chopped fresh dill

Beat the butter until soft, then beat in the salt, pink peppercorns and dill. Place in a ramekin, or roll into a sausage using a strip of baking paper, twist the ends to secure, and refrigerate until firm.

Seaweed butter

This is a briney, funky, sweet-savoury butter that is, unsurprisingly, fantastic with seafood, but it also brings an extra dimension to steamed potatoes or vegetables, or just smeared thickly on wholemeal bread.

1 nori sheet

75g butter, soft

Using scissors, cut the nori sheet into very small pieces. Beat the butter until soft, then beat in the nori pieces. Place in a ramekin, or roll into a sausage using a strip of baking paper, twist the ends to secure, and refrigerate until firm.

Cacio e pepe butter

Marmite butter

Freshly ground black pepper and aged Italian cheese is a Roman staple for a reason: sharp and rich, spicy and earthy, it will lift and enhance anything you put it on. It is the Chanel No. 5 of butters.

I don't think I really need to sell Marmite to you: its distinctive, salty, savoury flavour is legend. Combining it with butter mellows it and makes it more spreadable or pourable, which opens up the Marmitey possibilities. It will bring an extra dimension to your vegetables, especially leafy, green brassicas (and will change your Brussels sprout game entirely), can be used to toss potatoes in, should be drizzled over popcorn, and spread on the outside of toasties before toasting.

75g unsalted butter, soft

1 tablespoon finely grated pecorino

¼ teaspoon flaky salt

1 teaspoon freshly ground black pepper

Beat the butter until soft, then beat in the cheese, salt and pepper. Place in a ramekin, or roll into a sausage using a strip of baking paper, twist the ends to secure, and refrigerate until firm.

75g unsalted butter, soft

2 tablespoons Marmite

Beat the butter until soft, then beat in the Marmite until completely combined. Place in a ramekin, or roll into a sausage using a strip of baking paper, twist the ends to secure, and refrigerate until firm.

CHAPTER 2
BUTTER + EGGS

Butter and eggs

Combining butter and eggs is true kitchen magic: there are so many different ways to do it, each subtly different from the last, and each resulting in a completely different outcome.

Some of the simplest pleasures in the kitchen are brought about by combining butter and eggs: from an omelette, cooked in a scalding, buttery pan to slip-slidey eggs fried in brown butter flavoured with herbs or spice or other delicious nuggets – a different beast to the hot hot hot oil-fried crispy, lacy fried eggs you may be used to.

A breakfast of Turkish eggs, the yolks mixing with cool yoghurt and fiery spices, served in bed to the one you love, or presented to the whole table after a big night, to ease even the grimmest hangover.

When I was at university, I used to eat scrambled eggs almost every day for lunch. I'd make them in the microwave, then turn out the jellied, rubbery mass on to some cheap toast, garnish with a generous squirt of ketchup, and pat myself on the back, eating them over whatever Spenser or Milton I was trying and failing to understand. The quality of those scrambled eggs matched the essays I used to write.

My scrambled eggs have improved over the years, thank goodness, even if my understanding of courtly poetry hasn't. Now my scrambled eggs are cooked slowly (in a pan, over direct heat, for God's sake, Olivia), until they're custardy, soft, tender, and impossibly buttery.

But it's not just the simple stuff: some of the most technical bits of cookery are achieved by the simple combination of eggs and butter. Classical French sauces like creamy-tart hollandaise and my favourite, the bittersweet, anisey béarnaise, get their satiny, glossy textures and rich, rounded flavour from adding melted butter slowly, slowly to egg yolks, while cooking them. Those emulsions can be intimidating; they can take a while to get the knack. And if you get them wrong, you end up with a curdled, splitting, greasy mess. But what if that wasn't the case? What if there was a way of making these glorious sauces without the risk? Well, there is, it's ridiculously straightforward, and I'm going to share it with you.

And the eggs and butter relationship isn't just a savoury one, either. One of the first things I ever cooked was a lemon curd: I'd love to say that first experience of making curd was a reward in patience and faith, but to be honest, I was convinced I'd buggered it up. The eggs, lemon juice and butter take a bloody age to transform from a thin, watery liquid into something that can bear its own weight. Just at the moment when you're ready to give it up as hopeless, it comes good: thick, smooth, perfect. The first time that happened to me, I felt like a kitchen witch.

I love waves of my lemon curd simply piled on to toast – soft and silky but shouting with flavour, a completely different beast to those you can find on a

Turkish eggs with yoghurt and chilli butter

Turkish eggs are one of my very favourite breakfasts. Çılbır is a dish that dates back as far as the fifteenth century: poached eggs sit on top of garlicky yoghurt with feathery fronds of dill. Spooned over the top is browned butter flecked with Aleppo pepper. The brick-red Middle Eastern pepper isn't terribly hot, but is full of flavour; it tastes a little fruity, a little like cumin. The spiced butter may seem like a small part of the dish, but it pulls the whole thing together.

For a breakfast that is literally built on yoghurt, it is robust – but it's delicate too, the wispy, anisey dill brings freshness, while the acidic yoghurt balances the eggs and butter.

Makes: Breakfast for 2

Hands-on time: 15 minutes

Total time: 15 minutes

1 small clove of garlic, peeled

150g Greek yoghurt

½ tablespoon finely chopped fresh dill

¼ teaspoon salt

½ tablespoon lemon juice

½ tablespoon white wine vinegar

2 eggs, cracked into separate cups

25g salted butter

1 teaspoon Aleppo pepper

fresh dill, to garnish

1. Finely grate the garlic into the yoghurt, stir together with the dill, salt and lemon juice, and set to one side.

2. Bring a large pan of water up to a simmer, add the vinegar, swirl the water, and drop the 2 eggs into it, one at a time. Poach for 4–5 minutes, until the whites are set.

3. While the eggs are poaching, melt the butter in your smallest pan. Take it to the point where it is just starting to brown: it should smell nutty, but the colour won't really have changed yet. Stir in the Aleppo pepper, and set to one side.

4. Divide the yoghurt between two dishes, drain the eggs and set them on top of the yoghurt, dress with the butter and garnish with extra dill. Serve with warm, soft bread.

Hollandaise

Hollandaise is a dreamy sauce. For my money, it's one of the most sophisticated, elegant ways to eat butter: satin-smooth, thin enough to dribble off the spoon, but thick enough to enrobe whole eggs like a delicious cloak.

Traditionally, we serve hollandaise as part of eggs Benedict: poached eggs, sitting on top of ham on top of toasted English muffins. There are variations: eggs royale with smoked salmon in place of ham, or eggs Florentine, with spinach. But it's great with lightly steamed green veg (especially asparagus and Tenderstem broccoli), or little boiled new potatoes.

For all its virtues, hollandaise can be a tricky bastard. It's an emulsion (see page 86), so what you're trying to achieve is lots of butter molecules suspended in the water particles of the egg yolks and lemon juice. This is done by slowly cooking the egg yolks while gradually adding melted butter. It will thicken as it emulsifies into a lustrous, pourable sauce that is jam-packed with butter, but somehow doesn't feel greasy. But because it's an emulsion, it can break, and leave you with a pool of oil and a clag of egg yolk. So, how to avoid that?

Traditionally – classically – hollandaise is made by heating the butter and eggs over a terribly gentle heat, and whisking like mad. But! There is another way.

I've vacillated back and forth about whether to give you the 'traditional' way of making hollandaise, or the foolproof way. Eventually, the thought of a curdled hollandaise (all that butter, wasted!) is almost too much to bear. So, I'm going with the foolproof way: this way of making the sauce doesn't heat the egg yolks at all, but instead takes the butter to a much higher temperature. It then uses a stick blender or food processor to quickly, quickly break up the butter and push it into the egg yolks. It's brilliant.

Oh, and the people who sniffily tell you that the 'proper' way is better just want you to know that they know how to make it. Smile beatifically and then put a whole spoonful of the stuff straight into your mouth.

Makes: 250ml sauce (enough for 4)

Hands-on time: 10 minutes

Total time: 10 minutes

3 egg yolks

1 tablespoon lemon juice

a small splash of hot water

200g unsalted butter

salt, to taste

1. First, place the egg yolks, the lemon juice and a small splash of hot water into a small food processor or a narrow cup or jar that will just fit your stick blender.

2. Melt the butter in a small pan until it is bubbling fast and reaches 90°C. Carefully but swiftly pour this into a small measuring jug.

3. Whizz the egg yolks, lemon juice and water briefly in the processor or with the stick blender. Slowly drizzle in the hot melted butter: you should see the sauce thicken. Keep going until you've added all the butter. If you're using a food processor, you may need to pause, scrape down the sides, then continue. Season with salt, taste, and season again if necessary. Decant into a serving dish, or pour thickly over poached eggs, steamed green veg, or boiled new potatoes.

If you swap the lemon juice for blood orange juice, you make Maltaise sauce, which is particularly lovely spooned over shellfish or steamed spring vegetables

A TAXONOMY OF BUTTER SAUCES

In the late nineteenth century in France, things were changing. The Revolution had torn France's rigid social structures apart. In its wake, dining moved from private residences to a new kind of kitchen, where anyone who could pay the bill was welcome: the restaurant. The style of service changed too. No longer were dishes brought to the table all at once. Instead, they arrived in ordered courses, which diners selected from menus. Restaurant kitchens were organised around this way of dining, with 'brigades' of cooks each responsible for a particular element: meats, pastries, sauces, and so on. We have Auguste Escoffier, born in 1846, to thank for much of this. Escoffier modelled his brigades on military regiments, where strict hierarchies and responsibilities brought order where there would otherwise be chaos. A restaurant where anyone could demand whatever they liked, at any time, called for just this kind of system, and it has remained the principal way of running a kitchen ever since.

In this new age of dining, sauces became critical. The sauce added to a dish could completely change its nature, imparting a new texture or flavour and, crucially, enabling you to easily expand your menu, and the role of saucier became a hugely respected one.

Two quick definitions. A sauce is a thickened liquid – so gravy is a sauce, but a vinaigrette or melted butter is not. Sauces can vary in thickness and texture, but they should all be able to coat the back of a spoon. A roux is fat and flour cooked together, commonly used to thicken a sauce. The most common is a butter-and-flour roux, the basis for Escoffier's *béchamel*, *velouté* and *espagnole*. But you are also making a roux when you make gravy by stirring flour into the fat and juices of your roasted chicken. In New Orleans, the dark roux essential for gumbo, which must be cooked for a long time to achieve the depth of colour and flavour, is made with oil.

Marie-Antoine Carême published his famous classification of sauces in 1833. He identified four 'grand' or master sauces – béchamel, espagnole, velouté and allemande – and many more 'petit' sauces. Escoffier built on Carême's work, rejigging the list as he rejigged the kitchen itself. The result was a set of 'mother' sauces that, according to Escoffier, underpinned all good cuisine, and from which any other ('daughter') sauce could be made. There have since been decades of scholarly debate about which were Escoffier's true mother sauces – was hollandaise a mother or a daughter sauce? did a translator deliberately, villainously sideline mayonnaise in favour of hollandaise? – but most people settle on five: *béchamel*, *velouté*, *espagnole*, *tomate* and *hollandaise*.

Of these five mother sauces, all but *tomate* use butter as a building block. (In Escoffier's day, even *tomate* was thickened with a butter-and-flour roux, but now we generally just cook the tomatoes down further.)

To make *béchamel*, you simply add milk to a butter-and-flour roux, and cook it into a smooth white sauce. It is the true workhorse of Escoffier's sauces, and easily the one that I use most in my kitchen. *Béchamel* is the basis of chicken and ham pies, lasagne, soufflés (page 60), the body of a Spanish croquette, or the filling for a croque monsieur. Add Gruyère and you have *sauce mornay*, add Cheddar and you have *sauce cheddar*, either can be used in a cauliflower cheese, macaroni cheese, fish pie, or just spooned over eggs, veg or fish. For *sauce cream*, add cream and lemon. Add softly cooked and then puréed onions for a *sauce soubise*, and for the bold *sauce nantua*, add cream, butter, paprika and diced shellfish.

If you add light (traditionally veal) stock to your roux, you make a *velouté*. Today we find velouté in lobster bisque, or American-style sausage gravy. The *velouté* spin-offs are less well known than those of *béchamel*: *sauce bercy* uses fish stock, shallots, white wine, and more butter; *sauce allemande* includes veal sauce, egg yolk, cream and lemon; *sauce supreme*, made with chicken stock, mushrooms and cream, is something like a Campbell's soup, although I'll never be able to visit France again after writing that. The fanciest iteration is *sauce cardinal*: fish stock, cayenne, cream, and lobster.

If you cook the butter in your roux until it is nut brown, and add brown stock, congratulations, you've made *espagnole*. Or – let's be honest – gravy. *Espagnole* is the mother of many seriously rich daughters: *sauce chasseur* (mushrooms, shallots, white wine, tomatoes), *sauce chateaubriand* (white wine, shallots, tarragon and lemon – like a dark *béarnaise*), *sauce bordelaise* (red wine, shallots, bay leaf and thyme). I could go on.

Instead of a roux, *hollandaise* (page 57) begins with butter and egg yolks. To that simple, fragile emulsion is added shallots, tarragon and vinegar for *sauce béarnaise* (page 59), whipped cream for *sauce mousseline,* orange juice and zest for *sauce maltaise,* and saffron for the criminally underused *sauce grimrod.*

Phew.

69 Potato rösti

70 The platonic baked potato

73 Marmite butter potatoes

74 Hasselbacks with kimchi and blue
    cheese butter

76 Mashed potatoes

79 Fondant potatoes

81 Dauphine potatoes

82 Lancashire butter pie

84 Potato pavé

Marmite butter potatoes

Baby potatoes, grilled until charred and a little bit sticky, then coated with Marmite butter. What on earth could you want more than that? You can use different compound butters here, too – try the potatoes with chipotle butter (page 93), or cacio e pepe butter (page 32).

Serves: 4

Hands-on time: 5 minutes

Total time: 20 minutes

750g small/baby, waxy potatoes

60g butter

2 tablespoons Marmite

1 tablespoon balsamic vinegar

1. Preheat the grill to medium–high. Place the potatoes in a saucepan, cover with water, bring to the boil, reduce to a simmer and cook until tender, about 10 minutes. Drain the potatoes and transfer them to a roasting tin.

2. Grill the potatoes until charred and crisp, about 5–8 minutes, shuffling them regularly.

3. Melt the butter and Marmite together, then stir through the vinegar. Drizzle the butter into the roasting tin, then shuffle and toss the potatoes to coat them evenly in the butter, and slightly break the potatoes up. Return the glazed potatoes to the grill for 2 or 3 minutes, until they are burnished.

Hasselbacks with kimchi and blue cheese butter

The key to a good hasselback in my book is to fit in as many slices as you can (making them look, as Felicity Cloake says, like oversized woodlice). To aid you in making the multiple fine cuts you need for a beautiful hasselback, place the potato on a wooden spoon, and cut down the potato with a sharp knife: the curve of the spoon will allow you to make deep cuts without cutting right through the potato.

Cutting the potatoes in this way, and increasing the surface area literally and figuratively, opens them up to flavoured butters: the butter can get right down inside the crisped potato slices, coating them. The kimchi and blue cheese butter sounds like it might be much too much, but melted and bubbling between the crisp potato fins, it is just the right amount of salty sharp cheese and sour pickle – though these are a great vehicle for many compound butters. Try chicken skin butter, cacio e pepe butter, or a classic herb butter (see pages 27–35).

Serves: 4

Hands-on time: 10 minutes

Total time: 1 hour 5 minutes

8 medium King Edward potatoes

50g butter

100g Stilton

50g kimchi

1. Preheat the oven to 220°C.

2. Place a potato on a wooden spoon, and cut deep slices into it all the way along, without cutting all the way through. Repeat with the rest. Line a baking tray with tin foil, and place the potatoes on it. Melt 10g of the butter and brush it on to the top of each of the potatoes. Bake for 1 hour.

3. Blend together the remaining butter, the Stilton and kimchi in a food processor, and spread it on to the tops of the potatoes, which should now be splayed. Bake for 5 more minutes, then serve.

Mashed potatoes

It's a cliché to dislike lumpy mash, one that I wish I didn't subscribe to. I'd like to be carefree about my potatoes; I think it would make me appear both more laid back and cosily domestic if I proclaimed my love for the lump. But it's not to be: I really, really want completely smooth mash.

But, it has to be *mash*. I may be struck down by the culinary gods, but I'm not really interested in pommes purée, even though they're packed with my beloved butter. In fact, mash is a good example of the fact that, as wonderful as butter is, ploughing as much as you can into a dish isn't the answer. If I wanted to eat unadulterated butter, I think we all know I would. Joel Robuchon's legendary pommes purée have an almost 1:1 ratio of potato to dairy, and 200g of butter for every 500g of potato. But it's too much, and demands fine dining portions; when it comes to mash, I want a whole bowl of the stuff and a spoon, not artfully piped blobs. I want mashed potatoes that you can eat with a spoon, *and* stand a spoon up in.

Don't get me wrong, my mashed potatoes are still buttery. Extremely buttery. They're rich and smooth and indulgent and comforting, sweet and salty and creamy. But when it comes to mash, I want velvet, not silk. I want my mash to have body.

I like to pass my potatoes through a ricer to make sure they're really smooth, but I am easily bored and have zero upper body strength, so if you're willing to put in the effort to make it lump-free, a masher is absolutely fine – just don't be tempted to use a stick blender or food processor: you will break down the starch, turning the potatoes gluey.

Mashed potato is obviously a brilliant dish without any fiddling, but it's also a fantastic canvas for different flavours or additions. Try using smoked butter for a fantastic campfire flavour, or try browning the butter before beating it into the mashed potatoes, making them speckled, nutty, rich, and ultra buttery.

Dauphine potatoes

These, my friends, are potato doughnuts. That's right. I didn't come here to mess around. Not to be confused with potato dauphinoise, potatoes dauphine combine mashed potato with a choux pastry, and are fried in hot oil until they plump into feather-light potatoey puffs. Inside, pure mashed potato bliss; outside, blistered, deep-fried salty potato skin goodness.

Makes: 24 little potato doughnuts

Hands-on time: 30 minutes

Total time: 1 hour

300g baking potatoes, peeled

40g butter

For the choux

120ml water

50g butter

1 teaspoon fine salt

70g plain flour

2 eggs, beaten

2 litres vegetable oil, for frying

flaky salt

For the Coronation mayonnaise

½ a clove of garlic

200ml mayonnaise

1 teaspoon Dijon mustard

½ a lemon, juiced

1 teaspoon curry powder or garam masala

½ tablespoon mango chutney

a fistful of fresh coriander, finely chopped

1. Put the potatoes into a large pan, cover with water and bring to the boil. Cook until the potatoes are tender, and slide off the tip of a knife. Leave until cool enough to handle, then peel, cut into rough chunks and return to the pan. Run the potatoes through a ricer, so that they are completely smooth, then heat gently for a couple of minutes to drive off any moisture. Beat the butter into the mash.

2. While the potatoes are boiling, you can make the choux: heat the water, butter and salt in a small pan until the butter melts, and the whole thing reaches a rolling boil. Add the flour in one addition and beat to combine. Cook for another minute or so until the mixture sizzles on the bottom of the pan, then decant into a bowl.

3. Once slightly cooled, add the beaten eggs in small increments until combined. Pick up a dollop of the batter on your spatula and shake it off: if what remains on the spatula drops down in a deep 'V' shape, you have added enough egg; if not, add a little more and test again. Beat the mashed potato into the choux, and decant the mixture into a piping bag.

4. Heat the oil in a high-sided wide pan until it reaches 180°C, and line a plate with kitchen paper. Pipe out little nuggets of the potato-choux mixture and drop gently into the hot oil.

5. Deep-fry in batches in the oil, cooking for 3 minutes until golden and puffed. Use a slotted spoon to transfer them to the kitchen paper to drain for a couple of minutes. Sprinkle with flaky salt and enjoy hot. You can keep these warm in a low oven.

6. To make the mayonnaise, finely grate the garlic into the mayonnaise, then stir through the mustard, lemon juice, curry powder or garam masala and mango chutney. Decant the mayonnaise into one serving bowl, and sprinkle with coriander, and serve the potato doughnuts piled up in another serving bowl.

Lancashire butter pie

You have to hand it to us Northerners, we know how to make the most of a potato. Lancashire's butter pie has been a staple of the Preston area for centuries. Preston has always had a large Catholic community, and Catholics don't eat meat on Fridays – so in Preston, they eat butter pie. Or, as it is also sometimes known, Catholic pie or Friday pie. Now it is sold throughout pubs and shops, but is most frequently enjoyed as a match day half-time favourite at Preston North End football club.

It is, quite simply, a pie filled with potatoes, onion and butter; it has flaky pastry on the base, sides and top, and given the simplicity of its contents, a generous amount of salt and pepper. It is traditionally eaten with braised red cabbage.

Serves: 6

Hands-on time: 20 minutes

Total time: 2 hours

For the pastry

75g butter

75g lard

350g plain flour

1 teaspoon fine salt

75ml very cold water

For the filling

3 large potatoes, peeled and cut into slices

120g butter

2 large onions, cut into slices

salt and freshly ground black pepper

1 egg, beaten, to glaze

1. First, make the pastry. Rub the butter and lard into the flour and salt with your fingertips, until the mixture resembles breadcrumbs. Add the water, and cut it into the mixture with a knife. Once the dough starts to come together, use your hands to briefly knead the pastry, and make sure there are no dry bits. Wrap in clingfilm and rest in the fridge for an hour.

2. While the pastry is resting, boil the potato slices for 10 minutes, drain and set to one side. Heat 50g of the butter in a pan and cook the onion slices for about 10 minutes, until soft, but not coloured.

3. Preheat the oven to 180°C. Take two-thirds of the pastry and roll it out into a rectangle the thickness of a pound coin; use this to line a pie dish approximately 20 x 30cm. Layer the potatoes in the base of the pie, followed by the onions, then dot the remaining butter on top. Season liberally with salt and pepper. Roll out the final third of pastry into a rectangle the same size as the pie dish and place on top, using a fork to attach the pastry lid to the rest of the dish.

4. Brush the lid of the pie with egg wash, and stab a couple or so vent holes in the pastry with a knife. Bake for 30 minutes, until the pastry lid is firm and golden-brown.

physical contact (I never thought I'd feel so empathetic towards a hypothetical chemical, but here we are) – this means, in practice, that unless you force them to do otherwise, they will sit in unbroken layers.

So, to overcome this, you need to exert physical energy: whether that's through whisking, or beating, or shaking, or using a food processor or stick blender – or just shuffling the pan noisily.

What makes an emulsion far more likely to succeed is the presence of emulsifiers. These are molecules which will coat the surface of the added droplets and protect them from the surrounding liquid. They need to be soluble in both liquids, and they act like a bridge between the two, getting in the way of the other molecules. The emulsifiers we use most commonly in sauces are the proteins found in egg yolks and milk.

Temperature is often critical with butter emulsions. Too cold and the butter will solidify, breaking the emulsion; too hot and fat droplets will leak out, making the sauce greasy. If there are eggs in the emulsion, their proteins will coagulate at high temperatures too, the result being scrambled eggs.

But as ever in cooking, it depends on what you're trying to do. Heat can also create emulsions, which is why you don't want a stock to boil when you're clarifying it, as the fat will simply re-emulsify into the liquid. The same is true when clarifying butter (page 40). And it is this bit of knowledge that we take advantage of and turn on its head on page 165 for a foolproof cacio e pepe. Here, we boil together the butter and the pasta water, and the force of the roiling boil pushes the butter's fat molecules to disperse into the water, which forms a stable emulsion.

So, when you're whisking a beurre blanc, or a custard, or trying your hand at making butter, know that you're making (or breaking) an emulsion, and that that uncomfortable coalition is an ephemeral thing, a temporary liaison. And, to my chagrin, butter will thicken any water-based sauce if melted into it – try it with pan juices, or shuffled with pasta water – as long as you shake the pan with enough cheffy vigour.

92   Roast chicken with absolutely loads of butter

93   Lamb chops with chipotle and coriander butter

94   Butter shroud turkey

96   Butter-basted rib-eye steak

99   Old school chicken Kiev

100 Chicken liver pâté

102 Buffalo chicken wings

104 Wiener schnitzel

CHAPTER 4
BUTTER + MEAT

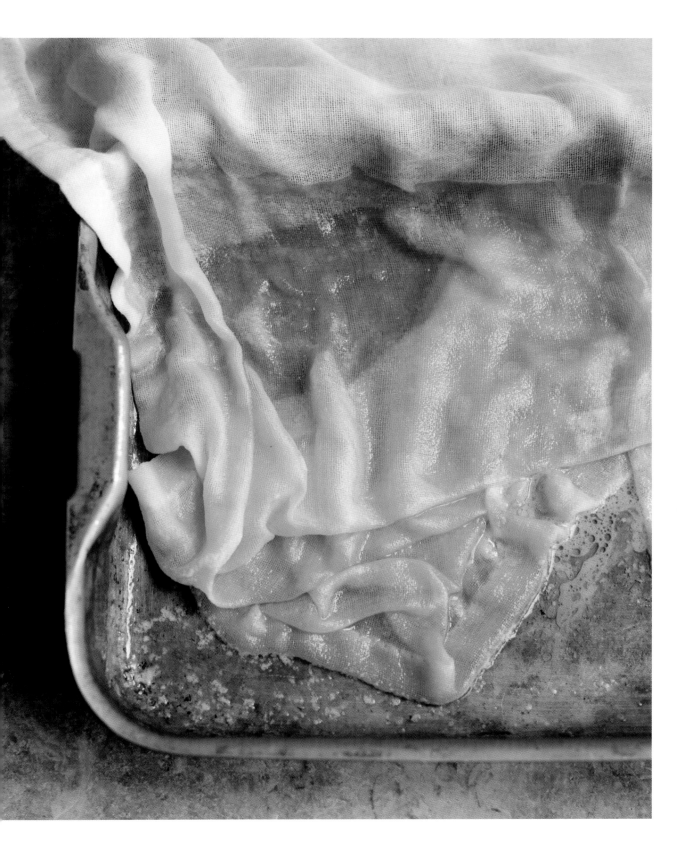

Butter-basted rib-eye steak

There is no better way to cook a steak than in a searingly hot pan, spooning hot, aromatic butter over the top. As the butter gently browns, the steak cooks fast on the outside and gently within, leading to that platonic ideal of a steak: crusted, mahogany, rich and salty on the outside, while still tender within.

I like my steak rare, but if you like yours well done, that's absolutely fine – food should be enjoyed by the person eating it, not by the ideals of the cook. But there's a difference between well done steak and overcooked steak. I use a temperature probe when cooking my steak: a deeply unsexy way of cooking, but one that ensures that I serve up extremely sexy, perfectly cooked, steak. You can cook your steak whichever way you want, I'm not here to police how you enjoy your food, but I will always be an advocate for making sure that you are actually cooking it how you'd like to eat it. So invest in a probe, it will pay dividends. And don't worry about stabbing it into the meat; it's a myth that the steak will lose all its moisture through a couple of judicious stabs. Similarly, flipping repeatedly ensures even cooking: so ignore anything telling you that you have to leave the steak untouched so that the crust forms; it's just not true.

This method will work for all steaks, but is by far the best for a bone-in, really thick steak, as you'll be able to build up a crust before the inside reaches your desired temperature; it is far better to have one thick steak cut between two of you.

I've kept it simple here with 'normal' butter, but this is where interesting butters come into their own: cultured butter, smoked butter, bourbon butter used from fat-washing, butter with spice and herbs packed into it, or butter salty with anchovies or chicken skin. I love cooking, but I also love being able to sit down with my friends when I feed them, and flavoured butters act as ready-made sauces for steaks – try butter with freshly crushed black peppercorns through it, the béarnaise butter on page 30, or go classic by serving your steak with a thick coin of Café de Paris butter (page 33).

Buffalo chicken wings

I always assumed that buffalo wings – those messy-sticky, spicy-sweet, crisp-tender nuggets – must be made of something desperately complicated, a secret sauce, maybe, in the manner of Coca Cola, where only three people in the world knew the full ingredients and they aren't allowed to travel on the same plane in case it crashed and the secrets died with them.

Turns out, I was very wrong: buffalo sauce is made up of three ingredients, butter, hot sauce and honey. That's it. The richness of the butter, the sweetness of the honey, and the vinegary tang and heft of spice from the hot sauce sit in perfect harmony. It tastes like so much more than three ingredients – but then, that's the power of butter.

These wings are oven-baked rather than deep-fried, but don't think that means compromise on texture or flavour. In fact, quite the opposite. These wings are great: the baking powder assists in the crisping and browning of the wings, and the initial low-and-slow bake allows the fat under the skin to render, while ratcheting the oven up and going hot hot hot ensures a combo of succulent meat and that nail-tapping glassiness that a good wing should have.

Makes: a big pile of wings (enough for 2 very greedy people, or 4 with other dishes)

Hands-on time: 20 minutes

Total time: 1 hour 20 minutes

1kg chicken wings, divided (see step 1 of method)

1 tablespoon baking powder

salt and freshly ground black pepper

To coat

60g butter

50g hot sauce

1 tablespoon runny honey

1. If you have whole chicken wings, you're best to divide them into wingettes (or flats), drumettes and wing tips. Holding the drumstick end of the wing, open out the wing at its main joint; using a sharp knife, cut through the flabby skin until you reach the joint. Place your knife tip in the hollow of the joint and cut through – the bones should separate pretty easily. Don't worry if you don't cut in exactly the right place. If your wings have wing tips on them, cut them off in the same way, going through the joint – discard the wing tips or use them for stock.

2. Preheat the oven to 120°C. Dry the chicken wings with kitchen paper, then toss the prepared wings in the baking powder, and season with salt and freshly ground black pepper.

3. Line a baking tray with tin foil and place an ovenproof rack on top. Space the wings on the rack in a single layer. Bake for 30 minutes, then turn the heat to 220°C and bake for a further 30 minutes.

4. In a small pan, melt the butter and then stir in the hot sauce and honey. Drizzle over the wings and toss to coat.

Dal makhani

Dal makhani is a feasting dish, often served at Indian weddings and celebrations. The name of the dish means 'buttery lentils', but that doesn't quite give a sense of the dark, smoky, complex flavours. It's a slow dish: the slow cooking of the lentils and dairy together is what gives the dish its richness and depth, and as the lentils begin to break down, they meld with the milk and then the butter to create a thick, intensely flavoured sauce. This freezes beautifully, and there are few things that can lift a bad day more effectively than pulling a portion of this from the depths of your freezer.

Serves: 8

Hands-on time: 1 hour

Total time: 12–24 hours

400g urad dal

2 onions, roughly chopped into chunks

8 cloves of garlic, peeled

5cm piece of root ginger, peeled

120g butter, divided into two equal amounts

100g tomato purée

2 teaspoons garam masala

2 teaspoons chilli powder

1 teaspoon fine salt

600–700ml whole milk

a fistful of fresh coriander, to serve

1. Place the dal in a colander or sieve and rinse under running water, until the water runs clear. Place the dal in a large bowl or pan and cover with 2 litres of water, then leave to soak for 6–16 hours.

2. Drain off the soaking water, place the dal in a large saucepan, and cover generously with fresh, cold water. Bring to the boil and cook for at least 2 hours, until the lentils are soft and can be crushed easily against the side of the pan.

3. Meanwhile, put the onions, garlic cloves and ginger into a food processor, and whizz to a very finely chopped consistency.

4. Melt 60g of the butter in a frying pan, and add the onion–garlic–ginger mix. Cook on low for 10 minutes, stirring regularly, until the mix is just starting to take on colour. Add the tomato purée, spices and salt, and cook, stirring, for another 5 minutes.

5. Once the lentils are cooked, drain off enough water so that the dal is covered by the water, but no more. Add 600ml of the milk and the spiced tomato mixture to the pan, stir thoroughly and bring to the boil, then reduce to a low simmer, stirring every 10 minutes.

6. After an hour, try the dal: if it isn't yet rich and darkly flavoured, add another 100ml of water and the remaining 100ml of milk, and cook for another 30 minutes, before checking again. This is less about reducing the liquid, and more about cooking the lentils until they break down and enrich the mixture, so don't be afraid to top up the liquid levels, and cook a little longer.

7. Once you're happy with the texture and flavour, stir through the rest of the butter, and taste for seasoning. Serve with torn coriander.

Green beans amandine

Green beans amandine – more correctly, *haricots verts amandine*, but it's just not as satisfying to say – is a classic French side dish, which makes use of a classic French technique. Cooking the nuts in butter helps them brown more easily, and makes it less likely that they'll burn, meaning that you can take them further than you could in a dry pan, so that they become deliciously, compulsively brittle. The green beans are blanched until cooked, but still snappy, added to the garlicky, shalloty, buttery almonds, along with a little lemon juice and a couple of tablespoons of water, and then the whole thing is agitated. Shaking the pan may not feel like very much is happening (although it does *look* quite cheffy, which is a bonus), but it is that shaking which helps the butter and water emulsify together (pages 86–7). Once emulsified, the sauce should be glassy and glossy, thicker than the butter alone, and not at all greasy: if it looks watery, keep heating and shuffling the pan; if it looks greasy, add a little more water.

You can top and tail the green beans, but I rather like the wiggly, tapering tails of the beans left untouched, just knocking off the very topmost tips where the beans were joined to the plant.

Although this technique is classically used with green beans (or the trout on page 135), it's fantastic with Tenderstem broccoli, halved sprouts, or baby radishes.

Makes: enough for 4 as a side

Hands-on time: 15 minutes

Total time: 15 minutes

320g green beans

25g salted butter

30g flaked almonds

1 banana shallot, thinly sliced

2 small cloves of garlic, thinly sliced

½ a lemon, zested and juiced

salt

1. First blanch the green beans in a large pan full of generously salted boiling water. Have a large bowl of iced water ready. Cook for 4–5 minutes, until the beans are tender, but still crisp – check by biting the end of one of them. Strain the beans into a sieve or colander, then immediately transfer to the iced water, then drain.

2. Melt the butter in a cast iron pan. Once the butter is bubbling, add the flaked almonds and sauté, stirring the whole time. Once the almonds are turning golden-brown, add the shallot and garlic. Sauté for 1–2 minutes more.

3. Transfer the blanched beans to the skillet and toss the ingredients together. Add the lemon juice and zest, and season with salt. Turn out on to a dish or platter, and serve.

Ukrainian burnt aubergine butter

I first learnt about aubergine butter from Ukrainian food writer and chef Olia Hercules's book *Summer Kitchens*, where she writes about it as a recipe she found in a Ukrainian cookbook from 1929. If you've had baba ghanoush before, this is similar, smoky and soft, with incredible depth – but without the tahini or garlic, the aubergine is very much the star of the show. It's lighter than baba ghanoush, and where olive oil would bring a touch of bitterness, the butter is mellow and sweet. I don't even really need a vehicle for this, I'm quite happy to eat it just by the spoonful. But, if pushed, I'm willing to load it on to flatbread.

Makes: 1 pot of aubergine butter

Hands-on time: 10 minutes

Total time: 20 minutes

1 aubergine

20g butter, soft

½ teaspoon flaky salt

1. First, burn your aubergine. Place the aubergine on the grate above a burner on a gas stove, and turn the burner to a high heat. Using tongs, turn the aubergine every couple of minutes until the entirety of the skin is blackened and crackled, and the flesh beneath is collapsing and soft. If you don't have a flame hob, you can achieve a similar effect using a grill: prick the aubergine all over with a fork, then place it under a medium grill, turning every so often until it's entirely soft.

2. Place the softened aubergine in a small bowl, cover with clingfilm, and leave until it has cooled enough to handle but is still warm. Remove the clingfilm, peel away the blackened skin and discard. Using a fork, mash the aubergine, including any juices that have come out of it, the butter and the salt together until combined.

COWS, *THE LAST SUPPER*, AND ELVIS PRESLEY: BUTTER SCULPTURE AND STATE FAIRS

Sometimes I worry that I elevate butter beyond its status. (Then I eat a freshly baked croissant, and quickly remember that, if anything, I am downplaying its brilliance.) But you may be surprised to hear that there are people even more obsessed than me. Let me tell you about the bizarre and wonderful world of American state fairs. This is a place where butter is taken extremely seriously.

25 million people attend state fairs in the US each year. They began life as agricultural shows: farmers would come along to exhibit their best pumpkins or hogs, for both pride and profit. Now they are major cultural events, with carnival rides and concerts and sports tournaments. A state fair can make or break a presidential run, as candidates jostle to kiss babies, gamely eat unlikely deep-fried foods, and win the endorsement of local kingmakers.

Among the most popular attractions at any state fair are the butter sculptures, which are exactly what they sound like: enormous statues modelled entirely from butter. The first one was carved for the Ohio State Fair in 1903. The butter came from a local creamery, and the sculpture was, essentially, an advertisement, but a wildly popular one, and butter sculpture quickly became a fixture at any fair worth its salt (so to speak).

Incredibly, outside of state fairs, butter sculpture has even older roots. Tibetan Buddhists have sculpted yak butter for centuries. There is archaeological evidence of butter carving in Ancient Rome and Babylon. During the Renaissance, butter art – alongside the better-known sugar art – would have served as the centrepiece to many a banquet. In 1536, Pope Pius V's cook, Bartolomeo Scappi, prepared a feast featuring butter sculptures including an elephant with a palanquin and Hercules wrestling the lion, which were paraded into the dining hall to the delight of the Pope's guests. In the mid-eighteenth century, Antonio Canova, a sculptor now better known for his more enduring marble creations, apparently won the attention of his first patron by sculpting a lion from butter when he was working as a kitchen boy.

In 1876, at the US's first World's Fair, Caroline Shawk Brooks, an Arkansas farmer's wife, exhibited Dreaming Iolanthe, a bas-relief depicting Yolanda, the heroine of the play King Rene's Daughter, sculpted from butter. Pre-refrigeration, the artwork had to be cooled from behind by a regularly replenished bowl of ice. Shawk Brooks had no training whatsoever in art or sculpture. She lived on a dairy farm, where she was in charge of butter production, and had first sculpted butter in 1867, 'the year the cotton crop failed'. It was common for dairy producers to press their butter into moulds, giving the butter pats distinctive or unique shapes. But Shawk Brooks began working freehand: she started small with faces and animals, as a means of promoting the butter she and her husband produced, but then was commissioned by a church fair to sculpt a large bas-relief of Mary, Queen of Scots. Dreaming Iolanthe was so popular that she never returned to Arkansas, and went on to formally train in sculpture in Paris and Florence.

In 1898, a monument to fallen troops was rendered in 500 pounds of butter at Minnesota State Fair, sponsored by a local dairy producer. But it was in 1903 that the first butter cow appeared at the Ohio State Fair, and tradition was really established.

At the early fairs, the sculptures tended to depict scenes from the dairy industry: cow and calf, milkmaids, or Greek and Roman images of agriculture and fertility. But like the fairs themselves, what began as a promotion of the dairy industry has become a celebration of Americana. The butter sculptures are now state fair attractions in their own right, and each year, brand new enormous structures – works of art – appear up and down the country, entirely made out of butter.

Butter sculpture is now a vocation, which demands a lifetime of work. From 1960 to 2005, Norma 'Duffy' Lyon, more commonly known as 'the Butter Cow Lady', was the official butter sculptor at Iowa State Fair. Starting in 1966, Lyon introduced a companion piece alongside her cow. These have included depictions of the Moon Landing, The Last Supper, Grant Wood's iconic American Gothic (my favourite), and life-size butter statues of Elvis Presley, Harry Potter, and characters from Star Trek and Sesame Street. Her endorsement of Barack Obama in the 2008 Iowa caucuses is said to have played a major role in his victory there, which ultimately helped Obama overcome the then favourite, Hillary Clinton, in securing the Democratic nomination.

At Iowa, the sculptures use anywhere from half a tonne to two tonnes of butter, provided by the event's sponsors, Southwest Dairy Farmers. It's a tricky medium – temperature control is crucial. And it's messy. The butter never sets in the way that other modelling materials would, so any knock or dint damages the sculpture. While the artwork may be ephemeral, the butter itself is not – as much as possible is reused year on year, sometimes for more than a decade. Sarah Pratt, the current resident sculptor and former apprentice of Norma, says that the butter she uses 'smells a lot like blue cheese'.

The Minnesota State Fair does things differently. Rather than depicting a dairy cow or Dolly Parton, their butter sculptor recreates the busts of the twelve finalists in that year's Dairy Princess competition – at the end of the fair, the finalists are given their likenesses carved in butter to take home with them.

And what if you turn up at a state fair actually wanting to eat butter, rather than just look at it? Fortunately, Abel Gonzels Junior – also known as 'the deep-fried Jesus' – has you covered. Deep-fried snacks, from corn dogs to funnel cakes, are a staple of all state fairs, but if Mr Gonzels is around you can also partake of deep-fried butter. It's sort of like a corn dog: a two-ounce stick of butter, battered and deep-fried for 3 minutes, then glazed. The batter is thick, and heavy with cinnamon and honey. Mr Gonzels's deep-fried dishes (he also invented deep-fried cola) are so popular that he makes enough money at the Texas State Fair to only work 24 days a year. The buttery dream.

135 Trout with buttered almonds

136 Grilled scallops with Seville orange and seaweed butter

138 Grilled kippers with horseradish butter

141 Roasted cod with beurre blanc

142 Sole meunière

144 Hot buttered lobster rolls

147 Oysters Rockefeller

148 Shrimp and grits

150 Louisiana seafood boil

Grilled kippers with horseradish butter

Serving kippers with butter is so much the norm that supermarkets now prepare them that way for you – the long, yellow fillets coming vac-packed with little flowers of butter to soak into the kippers as they cook. Generally they're meant to be microwaved or boiled in their packaging – but try grilling them, so that the flesh tightens and the skin crisps, and the butter browns under the heat of the grill. The sharp heat and accompanying sweetness of the horseradish can stand up to the bolshy flavours of a kipper, brightening and intensifying it.

Serves: 2

Hands-on time: 5 minutes

Total time: 10 minutes

50g butter

1 tablespoon creamed horseradish

2 kippers

1. Melt the butter in a pan and allow it to foam up and start to brown. Stir the horseradish through the butter.

2. Preheat the grill to medium-high. Line a high-sided tin with tin foil, and brush some of the horseradish butter over the tin foil. Place the fish, skin side up, on the buttered tin foil and grill for 1 minute, then turn them over, drizzle with the remaining horseradish butter, and grill for a further 5 minutes.

3. Serve the kippers hot, spooning any remaining horseradish butter over the fillets on the plates.

pot them. So if you're going to enjoy them, it's best to do so in small quantities and as an occasional treat. I toss them in hot melted butter, along with the spices traditionally found in potted shrimp, then spoon the whole thing on to dark bread: all the joy of potted shrimp, but in far smaller quantities, making it a more sustainable way to enjoy them. For two, melt 50g of butter in a small pan, and as it foams up, add ¼ teaspoon each of ground mace, ground white pepper and cayenne pepper, followed by 150g brown shrimp. Stir to warm through the shrimp, then tip on to bread, season with good salt and spritz with half a lemon.

If you fancy trying your hand at potting, I'd recommend potted rabbit or potted cheese. Rabbits continue to be plentiful, cheap and wild, and there's no better use for the remnants of a cheese board than potting them. For rabbit, joint the rabbit, and braise the pieces with 400g of rindless pork belly or bacon, and some aromatics – peppercorns, a couple of bay leaves, an onion, some thyme – until tender, about an hour. Leave to cool in the braising liquid, then strip the meat and the fat from the rabbit and the pork, stir together with a splash of the stock, and season to taste. Decant into clean, warm ramekins, pressing the mixture into the bowls. Clarify the butter, and add a small pinch of mace or nutmeg or allspice, and a little white pepper. Spoon the spiced butter over the meat, making sure that the contents of the bowls are completely covered.

For potted cheese, take 250g of whatever cheese you have left over or to hand, whizz it with 100g of soft butter, a splash of sherry and a splash of Worcestershire sauce in a food processor, spoon it into a ramekin, pressing it down to eliminate any air. Clarify a couple of tablespoons of butter, stir in a pinch of mustard powder, if you like; let it cool a little, and then pour it on to the surface of the cheese, making sure it's completely covered.

And in a waste-not, want-not frame of mind, we can take advice from Mrs Johnstone's 1826 *Housewife's Manual*. She advises 'what is left of the clarified butter (from potted lobster or crab) will be very relishing for sauces' and 'any butter from potted tongue or chicken remaining uneaten will afterwards be useful for frying meat and for pastry for pies'. My kind of woman.

158 Nigella's Marmite spaghetti

159 Buttery pilaf

160 Saffron and yoghurt tahdig

162 Sage butter fazzoletti

165 Cacio e pepe

169 Risotto Milanese

170 Risi e bisi

171 Garlic butter pull-apart dinner rolls

174 Buttered polenta

177 Jalapeño cornbread with honey butter

178 Singaporean kaya toast

180 Monte cristo

Sage butter fazzoletti

This is an incredibly simple way of dressing pasta, but also one of the best: butter is browned until nutty and speckled, then the hazelnuts and sage leaves are added to toast and crisp and flavour the butter. The cooked pasta is dropped into the buttery sauce, tossed briefly and served.

Of course, you needn't make your own pasta to enjoy this – you could buy fresh lasagne sheets and cut them in half – but if you haven't done it before, it's a lovely place to start: fazzoletti means 'handkerchief', and these big squares of pasta don't require a pasta machine, or any fancy cutting. Their joy is in their oversized floppiness, soaking up the sage butter.

Buttered polenta

'When you see the words "delicious" and "polenta" in close proximity, you know the phrases "plenty of cheese" or "lashings of butter" can't be far away.' Niki Segnit, author of *Lateral Cooking*, nails the simultaneous appeal and bemused distaste for polenta in one neat phrase.

At its best, polenta is indescribably comforting, rich and naturally sweet, soft and luscious. At its worst, it's lumpy, bland, claggy and, quite frankly, hard work. As so often is the case (and I think we can agree, I am entirely unbiased in this whole pursuit), the difference is butter.

Polenta has nothing to hide behind: no spice, no herbs, no bells and whistles; its simplicity is its appeal. So it all turns on the butter, bringing the whole thing to life. It begs to be joined by rich tomatoey ragùs, dark, sticky mushrooms, or slowly cooked meaty stews, but spooned into a bowl, with a pat of butter sitting on top, eaten on the sofa, alone, is almost as meditative as the act of cooking polenta itself.

Serves: 4

Hands-on time: 55 minutes

Total time: 1 hour

500ml water

½ teaspoon fine salt, or 1 teaspoon coarse salt

100g polenta

60g butter, cut into cubes

1. Bring the water to the boil in a large saucepan, seasoning it with the salt. Add the polenta slowly to the pan, picking it up in handfuls and letting it fall through your fingers, whisking with the other hand – adding it too quickly can create lumps.

2. Cook until the mixture begins to thicken – around 5 minutes – stirring the whole time, then turn it down to the very lowest heat possible on your stove. Cook for 45 minutes, stirring and scraping the bottom every few minutes with a silicone spatula, until the polenta is very thick. Season to taste with more salt, if needed, then stir in 45g of the butter, beating the polenta vigorously until it is smooth and combined.

3. Serve with the remaining butter on top, melting into the polenta.

Treacle soda bread

'Quick' breads are a great use of buttermilk: the acid in the buttermilk reacts with the alkali in the bicarbonate of soda, which is what causes the rise in the bread. No yeast needed, and no proving either. The crumb is softer and looser than 'normal' bread, and it has a shorter shelf-life. And, of course, is only improved by thick, creamy butter. In a pinch, you can just use 100% plain flour, ditch the oats and the treacle, but this is my absolute favourite soda bread: dark, damp, nubbly and slightly sweet.

Makes: 1 loaf of soda bread

Hands-on time: 10 minutes

Total time: 45 minutes

200g plain white flour

200g plain wholemeal flour

100g jumbo oat flakes, plus extra for sprinkling

15g bicarbonate of soda

10g salt

400ml buttermilk

2 tablespoons black treacle

2 tablespoons runny honey

1. Preheat the oven to 200°C, and line a large (900g) loaf tin with a strip of baking paper.

2. Stir together the dry ingredients in a large mixing bowl. Add the wet ingredients and stir the mixture together briefly into a wet dough.

3. Spoon the mixture into the prepared loaf tin (it will be wetter than normal bread dough; don't worry!), smooth the top and sprinkle with a few extra oats. Drag a knife or a dough scraper along the length of the loaf to part it a little in the middle. Bake for 35 minutes, until the bread is risen, craggy and a rich brown – it should have a firm crust. When the bread comes out of the oven, cover with a damp tea towel for 10 minutes: this will help keep the loaf moist. This bread is best on the day of baking, but will still be fine the following day, and still great toasted on days 2 and 3 (not that it will last that long once you've tasted it).

191 Extremely trashy Mars Bar krispie bites

192 Salted chocolate, hazelnut and rye cookies

194 Sticky gingerbread

196 The only brownie recipe you will ever need

198 Brown butter, milk chocolate and pretzel blondies

200 Baklava

203 Anzac flapjacks

204 Hawaiian butter mochi cakes with rosemary

207 Salted caramel

208 Salt and pepper caramels

210 Ginger and sour cherry fudge

212 Almond butter toffee brittle

CHAPTER 8
BUTTER + SUGAR

Butter and sugar

Butter and sugar are so obvious a pairing that it seems silly to try to sell it to you. If you're anything like me, this is the bit of the book that you will use most anyway, perhaps even the chapter that you turned to first. You could write a whole book on the relationship between butter and sugar – many people have.

I know that I am only ever one successful loaf of bread, one impressive batch of choux, two correct answers in an episode of University Challenge away from taking myself far too seriously. Luckily, I'm surrounded by a husband, family and dog who like to keep me in my place. And I can say, hand on heart, that this is their favourite chapter of the book (OK, perhaps not the dog, she's got her eye on the meat chapter). These are the dishes that sit on my kitchen side, that I give to my husband and friends, that I love to cook, that I want to eat. These are the bakes that made me fall in love with baking, and were probably my introduction to really cooking with butter at all.

In Butter + Friction and Butter + Air, you'll find all the theory about the incorporation of butter into cakes and biscuits, how different methods produce different results. But here, it's all about the unadulterated joy of combining butter and sugar.

So this chapter is filled with recipes that unapologetically showcase the best of butter and sugar, recipes that needs lots of both (you need a whole pat of butter for the brownies and the flapjacks, and not much less for the blondies). But they're also filled with my own loves, recipes that I've been making and tweaking and remaking for years, bakes that satisfy my own, personal sweet tooth. Here, you'll find my rye and dark chocolate cookies (page 192), Anzac coconut flapjacks (page 203), my brownies (page 196), and browned butter, milk chocolate and pretzel blondies (page 198). If I say to you that 'extremely trashy Mars Bar bites' (page 191) is Sam's favourite recipe in the whole book, it perhaps gives you a flavour of how good they are, and how much I've wanted to hit him with a frying pan when he's rated them above homemade croissants, the silkiest hollandaise, and steakhouse-standard rib-eye.

But it would be wrong to have a butter and sugar chapter without a glimpse into the magic that can happen when you apply heat to the equation. Confectionery-making might also be all about butter and sugar, but it can feel quite far removed from making a Krispie cake. But the effect of heat on butter and sugar is a remarkable one: cooked to 118°C, you can make fudge, bubbled until toothsome, and then beaten with a wooden spoon to give it that distinctive slightly crumbly grain. Go further and take it up to 122°C and it turns into proper caramel, chewy but not sticky, caramel that will set in a tin, and can be cut into neat squares, and twisted in brown paper. Cooking the sugar even higher to 150°C produces buttery toffee, which will set hard and crack when hit. Butter toffee should be glossy and thin, and never chewy. Combining it with nuts makes brittle which – as well as being delicious – means that you can actually bite through it, without risking a tooth. Homemade sweets not only boast a longer shelf-life than other butter-led bakes thanks to their sugar content, but they also make beautiful and impressive gifts.

Baklava

I find making baklava quite a meditative act: the cutting of the cool, papery filo to a size that will fit in my tin, the painting of it with melted butter, until it relaxes into the layer below, building up and up to a layer of nut rubble, and then more layers on top. Once chilled, the uncooked baklava will be firm with butter; I have yet to find a more satisfying kitchen act than cutting that butter-firm pastry into lozenges. The hisssss of the syrup hitting the baklava and soaking through the layers, into the nuts, and holding the whole thing together, feels like a sigh of relief.

It will feel like you have too much syrup, but you really don't, and the layers need it, so keep going. For structural integrity, I borrow from the great Claudia Roden, and return my soaked baklava to the oven for 5 minutes. Sticky, flaky, crumbly, and perfumed with spice, orange blossom water and honey, this is a beautiful baklava.

Salted caramel

Salted caramel is absolutely bloody everywhere. Salted caramel vodka, salted caramel shower gel, salted caramel scented candles. Just thinking about it I can almost smell that synthetic scent. But real salted caramel, made just from sugar, butter and cream, cooked until thick and complex, is like nothing else: rich and smoky, gooey, sweet and bitter, with the salt doing what salt does best, enhancing all the other aroma and flavour compounds.

It has a hundred uses: sandwich it between sponge cakes, use it to fill doughnuts or macarons, beat it into buttercream or whip it into a ganache, or stir chopped nuts through it and drizzle it over ice cream – and it keeps for absolutely ages in the fridge.

Makes: one 225g jam jar of caramel

Hands-on time: 10 minutes

Total time: 30 minutes

150g caster sugar

120ml double cream

½ teaspoon flaky salt

20g butter

1. First, measure out all your ingredients. Cover the base of a pan with a little of the sugar, and place over a medium-high heat. As the sugar begins to melt, add a little more. Don't stir the sugar while it's melting, but you can nudge any dry bits into the wet spots to encourage it to caramelise. Continue until you have used all the sugar. The sugar should be a rich mahogany colour, and just beginning to smoke.

2. Remove the pan from the heat and add the cream a little at a time, stirring it into the molten sugar. Adding it bit by bit helps it to caramelise properly. It will bubble up as you add and stir it, so be careful. Return briefly to the heat and stir to remove any lumps, adding the salt.

3. Remove from the heat. Allow to stand for 2–3 minutes, then stir in the butter until combined. Leave to cool for 15 minutes, then decant into a sterilised jam jar.

Butterscotch is similar to caramel, but its defining feature is that it's made with dark soft brown sugar, rather than caster sugar. Some people make it all in one, without caramelising the sugar, but I tend to stick to the same method as caramel as a starting point, but with a higher proportion of cream, so it is more of a pouring sauce. Try 75g of dark soft brown sugar, 50g of unsalted butter and 150g of double cream. The robustness of the dark sugar means that it can stand up to strong flavours, so sometimes I switch out the salt for ½ teaspoon of white miso, stirring that into the butterscotch sauce.

Salt and pepper caramels

I used to be scared of making caramels, feeling like I wasn't in control of what was happening, that the sugar, rather than me, was in charge. I would look at recipes and methods for making them, and they would swim in front of me, incomprehensible and intimidating. But when I realised that chewy caramels are really just making a salted caramel and then cooking it to a high temperature, it demystified the whole process.

You can flavour caramels with a hundred different things: replace the double cream with fruit purée, or infuse the cream before using it; you can also use cultured or smoked butter in place of 'normal' butter to impart interesting notes and aromas. The freshly ground black pepper here is spicy, fruity and warm.

Makes: 30 caramels

Hands-on time: 15 minutes

Total time: 5–12 hours 15 minutes

250g granulated sugar

150ml double cream

100g butter

2 tablespoons runny honey

1 teaspoon freshly ground black pepper

½ teaspoon flaky salt

1. Oil a 23 x 12cm loaf tin, and line it with a wide strip of baking paper with grabbable ends. Make sure all your ingredients are weighed out and within arm's reach.

2. Heat the sugar in a large, heavy-based pan over a medium–high heat until the sugar melts. Don't stir it while it's melting, but you can nudge the dry bits of sugar into wet spots to encourage it to caramelise.

3. When the sugar is all amber, and starting to smoke, pour in the cream and whisk to combine: the caramel will bubble up at this point and may release a lot of steam, so be careful. Stir in the butter, honey and pepper, until melted and combined.

4. Cook the caramel over a medium–high heat until the mixture reaches 122°C – this should take roughly 5 minutes. Once it's at temperature, remove from the heat and carefully decant into the lined loaf tin. Leave to cool completely, ideally overnight.

5. Turn out the caramel on to a chopping board and use a sharp knife to cut into squares or rectangles. Sprinkle the flaky salt on to the individual caramels. Use small pieces of baking paper or cellophane to wrap the individual caramels.

A BUTTERCREAM PRIMER

When it comes to buttercream, butter is unsurprisingly king. But what is maybe more unexpected is the variation between different types of buttercream, and the way in which butter is incorporated into them. With bases ranging from custard, to meringue, to roux, there are all sorts of ways to make beautiful, luscious fillings for cakes, éclairs and pastries.

You can flavour buttercream with puréed fruit or fruit juice, with coffee or nut pastes, or spreads like peanut butter, Nutella or Biscoff. You can create a chocolate buttercream by adding cocoa powder or melted and cooled chocolate. If I'm making a buttercream that uses caster sugar, I like to use vanilla sugar. When you've made something using a vanilla pod, run the scraped pod under water, and dab it dry with kitchen paper. Pop it in a container filled with caster sugar, and let the perfume of the vanilla gently infuse and perfume the sugar.

Adding too much liquid can cause the buttercream to split, so the more you can concentrate a flavour – or a colour – the better. Gel or powder colourings are better than liquid colourings; their concentration means a stronger colour, and that you don't have to dilute the mixture.

If you've made the base of your buttercream properly, the most likely problem you'll encounter is temperature: if the buttercream seems too soft, a short spell in the fridge, followed by vigorous whisking or beating, will correct its texture; if it seems too hard, simply let it sit at room temperature for a while, then whisk or beat.

All the recipes on the following pages should yield enough buttercream to ice a 20cm cake, or 12 cupcakes.

American buttercream

This is the classic buttercream and the simplest of the lot: it's the one you learn to make when you're little, that you swipe off cupcakes with your finger, the one that sticks the wings on to butterfly cakes. With two parts icing sugar to one part butter, beaten together until fluffy, it is very sweet.

500g icing sugar

250g salted butter, soft

½ teaspoon vanilla paste

1–2 tablespoons whole milk

Sift the icing sugar into a large bowl. Beat the soft butter into the icing sugar, slowly at first to stop the icing sugar billowing everywhere, then quickly, once combined. Beat until very smooth, and paler in colour than when you started. Beat in the vanilla paste, and enough milk just to loosen the mixture a little.

Swiss meringue buttercream

This is a great buttercream (I use it for all my wedding cakes): it is 'non-crusting', which means it is incredibly smooth and stays glossy; it's also less sweet than American buttercream. Egg whites and sugar are cooked together to 85°C, then whisked to a stiff meringue. Soft butter is slowly added, until the meringue transforms from a soupy mess into a thick, beautiful frosting that ripples and swoops.

Its stability means it takes on flavour and colour well, but I often keep it simple. Swiss meringue buttercream is used for the browned butter sponge on page 253.

80g egg whites

160g caster or granulated sugar

¼ teaspoon fine salt

½ teaspoon vanilla paste

250g salted butter, really soft

Heat the egg whites, sugar, salt and vanilla paste together in a bain-marie (a heatproof bowl sitting on top of a pan of barely simmering water) until they reach 85°C. Pour the mixture into the bowl of a stand mixer, and whisk until the meringue cools down (the bowl should no longer feel warm) and forms stiff peaks. Add the soft butter in five separate additions. The mixture may appear to split as you add the butter, but by the time you've added it all, it should be thick and luscious.

Use the beater attachment to beat the buttercream for a few minutes (this knocks the air out of it, which means you can apply it more smoothly). If the buttercream is too loose, you can leave it in a cool place to firm up a bit – but don't forget about it, or it'll be too hard to apply.

Russian buttercream

Russian buttercream (also called condensed milk buttercream) makes me laugh, because it is basically just butter beaten into condensed milk, and I take my hat off to whoever invented it. The butter is whisked for ages to incorporate as much air as possible – which will make the buttercream taste smooth, and melt-in-the-mouth – and then the condensed milk is slowly added. A little vanilla and salt round it out and smooth the edges.

250g butter, soft
½ teaspoon fine salt
1 teaspoon vanilla paste
1 x 397g can condensed milk

Whisk the butter in the bowl of a stand mixer using a whisk attachment for 5 minutes, until very pale and fluffy. Add the salt and vanilla paste. Whisk in the condensed milk in five separate additions, fully incorporating each addition before the next. This buttercream doesn't like standing around as much as the others do, so aim to pipe or use it within the day.

Ermine buttercream

Ermine buttercream (also called boiled milk buttercream, which perhaps isn't the greatest marketing) is an old-fashioned, roux-based frosting. Unlike most of the other buttercreams, it's eggless, which makes it great for dietary requirements. With a texture like whipped cream, it was the original icing for red velvet cake.

115ml whole milk
20g plain flour
40g caster sugar
½ teaspoon vanilla paste
115g salted butter, soft

In a saucepan, whisk together the milk and flour over a medium heat until they thicken – this should take a couple of minutes. Stir in the sugar and vanilla paste, decant into a heatproof bowl, cover with clingfilm touching the surface, and leave to cool completely.

Beat the butter in a separate bowl until it is very soft, then add the roux mixture a little bit at a time, until the whole thing is combined and smooth.

Italian buttercream

French buttercream

Italian buttercream is a similar idea to Swiss meringue buttercream, only here the sugar is cooked into a syrup before it is poured into the egg whites. It is a little faffier to make than the Swiss variety, but it is ridiculously smooth and stable. You can substitute honey, maple syrup or golden syrup for the simple syrup, but be aware that they will reach higher temperatures faster than the sugar–water mix.

180g granulated sugar

60ml water

90g egg whites

½ teaspoon vanilla paste

300g salted butter, very soft

Put the sugar into a small, heavy-based pan with the water, and cook over a low heat until the sugar dissolves, then turn up the heat. When the syrup reaches 115°C, start whisking your egg whites in the bowl of a stand mixer. Once the syrup reaches 120°C, with the mixer running, pour it slowly into your egg whites (you're looking to pour straight down, missing the whisk itself and the sides of your stand mixer bowl; I find doing this from a height helps). Once you've added all the syrup, continue whisking on high speed until the mixture has cooled to room temperature. Add the vanilla paste, then add the very soft butter, 25g at a time, waiting for each addition to incorporate before adding the next; by the time you've added all the butter, the mixture should be glossy and thick.

French buttercream is similar to Italian buttercream, but instead of pouring the hot syrup on to egg whites, you pour them on to egg yolks – this is known as *pâte à bombe* – before beating in a boatload of butter. Using yolks rather than whites makes it rich and fragrant, but still remarkably light, and it doesn't need anything more than vanilla to flavour it. It is blonde rather than the white of the meringue-type buttercreams, thanks to the presence of the yolks.

180g granulated sugar

120ml water

6 egg yolks

300g salted butter, very soft

½ teaspoon vanilla paste

Place the sugar in a small, heavy-based pan with the water, and cook over a low heat until the sugar dissolves, then turn up the heat. When the syrup reaches 115°C, start whisking your egg yolks in the bowl of a stand mixer. Once the syrup reaches 120°C, with the mixer running, pour it slowly into your egg yolks (you're looking to pour straight down, missing the whisk itself and the sides of your stand mixer bowl; I find doing this from a height helps). Once you've added all the syrup, continue whisking on high speed until the mixture has cooled to room temperature. Add the very soft butter, 25g at a time, waiting for each addition to incorporate before adding the next; by the time you've added all the butter, the mixture should be glossy and thick. Add the vanilla paste and whisk again until just combined.

Crème mousseline

Crème mousseline (also called German buttercream) is a thick custard with lots of butter beaten into it. Vanilla, coffee or praline flavours are the most traditional – I use hazelnut mousseline in the Paris-Brest on page 260 – but you could also replace the milk with fruit juice, or infuse the milk with whole spices or herbs, like cardamom or bay, to flavour the buttercream.

Whisk the cooled crème pâtissière in a stand mixer or by hand (it will be quite jellyish when you decant it from the bowl, but will become luscious and smooth as you whisk it). Add the very soft butter in four additions, beating each thoroughly into the mixture before adding the next. The finished mousseline will be beautifully silky and thick.

½ a vanilla pod, or 1 teaspoon vanilla paste

250ml whole milk

3 egg yolks

100g caster sugar

35g cornflour

125g salted butter, very soft

Split the vanilla pod using a small, sharp knife, and scrape out the black seeds, if using. Place the seeds and empty pod (or vanilla paste, if using) in a medium-sized saucepan with the milk, and bring to steaming. Whisk together the egg yolks and caster sugar in a bowl until they are pale and thick; whisk in the cornflour.

Fish out the vanilla pod from the milk and set to one side (you can wash and dry this and use it to make the vanilla sugar used on page 215). Pour a little of the steaming milk into the egg yolk mixture, whisking until the mixture is loose enough to pour back into the pan. Return the pan to the heat, and whisk constantly until the mixture is very thick and you can see bubbles coming up through the mixture (the mixture needs to boil for the cornflour to lose its floury taste). Decant immediately into a clean, heatproof bowl, cover the surface with clingfilm, cool and refrigerate until cold.

224 Perfect scones

226 Cultured butter and vanilla shortbread

228 Ploughman's quiche

229 Rye treacle tart

230 Tarte au citron

232 Boozy black cherry frangipane tart

235 Earl Grey chocolate tart with chocolate pastry

238 French salted butter biscuits

240 Parmesan and black pepper sablés

243 Breton cake

244 Tartiflette galette

Makes: one 23cm tart
(serves 6–8)

Hands-on time: 30 minutes

Total time: 4 hours

For the pastry

50g icing sugar

125g butter, soft

¼ teaspoon fine salt

½ teaspoon vanilla paste

1 egg yolk

160g plain flour

20g cocoa powder

For the filling

240ml double cream

125ml whole milk

3 tablespoons loose-leaf Earl
Grey, or 3 Earl Grey teabags

2 tablespoons dark soft brown
sugar

¼ teaspoon salt

½ teaspoon vanilla paste

250g dark chocolate, chopped

2 egg yolks

1. Make the pastry. Sift the icing sugar into a stand mixer or large bowl. Cream the icing sugar with the butter, then add the salt and vanilla paste. Beat in the egg yolk, followed by the flour and cocoa powder. Beat briefly until smooth, then turn out on to a sheet of clingfilm, wrap and flatten into a disc, and freeze for an hour.

2. Meanwhile, infuse the cream for the filling. Heat the cream and milk with the loose-leaf tea or tea bags until little bubbles appear at the edge of the pan. Turn off the heat, leave to infuse for 30 minutes, then strain the cream to remove the tea, pressing the tea leaves or bags gently.

3. Remove the dough from the freezer and grate it coarsely on to a plate. Scatter the grated pastry across your tart tin (I use a shallow 23cm fluted tin, but there is some wiggle room here), mounding it a little on the sides. Using your fingertips, press the pastry together to form an even layer, and a flush border. Prick the base of the pastry all over with a fork, and refrigerate for 20 minutes.

4. Preheat the oven to 170°C. Line the pastry case with oven-safe clingfilm or baking paper, and fill to the brim with dry rice or baking beans. Bake for 15 minutes. Remove the clingfilm/paper and rice/baking beans, and bake for another 5 minutes, until the pastry is dry. Turn the temperature down to 150°C.

5. To finish the filling, stir the brown sugar, salt and vanilla paste into the infused cream and milk mixture, then bring back up to a simmer. Place the chopped chocolate in a heatproof bowl, and pour the cream and milk over the top. Leave for 2 minutes, then stir until combined. Whisk in the egg yolks, then pour the whole thing into the cooled tart shell. Bake for 15 minutes, until the filling is set and glossy. Leave to cool completely in the tin before demoulding, slicing and serving.

French salted butter biscuits

These biscuits come from Brittany, in northern France, a region which has had a huge influence on all types of pastry, thanks to its production and love of butter, salt, and crucially, salted butter. Sablé Breton is a salted butter biscuit dough, with a high proportion of butter, sugar, and egg yolk. The biscuits are a pain to handle, sticky and tricky to move once cut, but also entirely worth it. Sablés Bretons are predictably rich, crisp, crumbly and impossibly buttery.

You can use the dough as an incredibly elegant and rich base for a pudding, in lieu of other pastry, but it will stand proudly alone, baked up as individual biscuits – I love them dunked in a cup of strong coffee.

You can make these without a muffin tin, but you'll need to refrigerate or freeze the cut dough before baking, to stop them spreading too far on your baking tray.

Many of the supermarkets now stock different types of butter; if you can get Brittany butter for this, use it and omit the extra salt in the dough recipe.

Makes: 20 biscuits

Hands-on time: 20 minutes

Total time: 1 hour 35 minutes

2 egg yolks

100g caster sugar

100g unsalted butter, soft

135g plain flour

1½ teaspoons baking powder

1 teaspoon coarse salt

1 egg yolk, to glaze

1. In a stand mixer, whisk together the egg yolks and sugar until the mixture is pale and visibly increased in volume. Whisk in the butter, bit by bit. Turn the mixer down to low, then incorporate the flour, baking powder and salt.

2. Scoop the mixture out on to a piece of baking paper (it will be very sticky and wet), and cover with a second piece of baking paper. Roll out the dough between the sheets to 1cm thick and refrigerate for at least an hour.

3. Preheat the oven to 160°C. Carefully remove the top layer of the baking paper from the dough. Brush the entire sheet of dough with egg wash, then drag a fork across the dough on the diagonal to create a criss-cross pattern. Cut out as many 5cm rounds as you can from the dough. Return any spare dough to the fridge, to re-roll and cut later. Carefully transfer each round into a muffin hole, and bake for 15 minutes. Leave to cool, then lift from the muffin tin (you may need a knife to help lift them).

Because of the air incorporated into the dough by creaming, it's particularly important with creamed pastry doughs to make sure that the pastry is properly weighed down with pastry weights when you blind bake it, so that it doesn't inflate while it's cooking.

Flaky, rough puff, galette, pie pastry and American biscuit dough

When you make any of these pastries, your aim is the opposite of that of the rubbing method: you want to make sure you're incorporating whole lumps of butter. Some recipes will tell you to take the butter to the size of small peas, but I think that's still too small. I aim for about half the butter pieces being pea-sized and the rest chickpea-sized; as you roll out and shape or fold the pastry, those pieces of butter will inevitably get smaller. The water content from the little lumps of butter creates steam in a hot oven, which forces the dough above it to rise, thus creating pockets and flakes in the pastry or dough.

'Proper' puff pastry and croissant dough

For laminating puff pastry and croissant dough, you're using a whole butter block, which you've beaten into a shallow slab. As this butter block is folded into the dough, it is stretched, and becomes thinner, forming many layers of butter sitting in between layers of dough. When the heat of the oven hits the dough, the butter melts and produces steam, pushing and separating out the distinct layers of dough, and giving the pastry its height.

If you weigh down the puff pastry with another flat tray when baking it, the butter will melt and create steam, but the layers won't be able to puff upwards: you'll end up with layers that are still defined, but compressed, and even flakier than normal puff – this is great for dishes like mille-feuille where you don't want the pastry to become unwieldy.

Developing the gluten

While you're doing everything you can to guard against gluten development when making pastry, biscuits and cakes, the opposite is true when making an enriched dough, like brioche or bun dough. You need to develop the gluten by giving it a good knead before you add the butter to it, otherwise the butter will inhibit gluten development.

Chill out

When you're laminating butter into a base dough, for croissants or puff pastry, the butter needs to be cold enough that it's not going to melt or smudge into the dough, but with enough plasticity that it won't crack or splinter as you roll and fold it.

Usually, with pastry or laminated dough, you rest it in the fridge at least twice: first when you've just combined it, and second when it's in its final pre-baking state. The gluten has time to relax, which means that, for pastry, the dough won't tighten and shrink as it bakes, and won't be so elastic that you can't roll it out as far as you need. If your dough is springing back on you as you try to roll it, return it to the fridge for another 20 minutes.

252 Quatre-quart cake

253 Burnt butter sponge with burnt buttercream

256 Honey and hazelnut friands

257 Welsh rarebit gougères

260 Paris-Brest with praline mousseline

262 St Louis gooey butter cake

263 Sweet and sticky saffron buns

264 Brown butter cinnamon rolls

266 Dark chocolate and tahini babka

269 Kardemummabullar

272 Rhubarb and custard doughnuts

276 Brioche

Paris-Brest with praline mousseline

Crème mousseline is a buttercream made from a thick pastry cream or custard, with a boatload of butter beaten into it. It is sometimes flavoured with vanilla or chocolate, but usually it is made with praline. It's also the traditional filling of a Paris-Brest, which is a choux pastry in the shape of a bicycle wheel, created by Louis Durand in 1910 to commemorate the Paris-Brest bicycle race.

Listen, I'm a food writer, I should be better than this, but I'm afraid it is impossible to adequately describe the deliciousness of praline crème mousseline, especially when sandwiched between crisp, choux shells. I'm sorry, but I cannot do justice to the light, hazelnut, custardy, buttery swirls. You'll just have to take my word for it, and make it.

Paris-Brest also uses butter in another way: the choux is usually topped with craquelin before baking. Craquelin is a simple butter-sugar-flour dough that you place on the raw choux like a little hat. It melts on to the choux as it bakes, encasing it, smoothing out any imperfections in your piping, and crackling into an attractive, biscuity crunchy top.

Makes: 4 choux wheels

Hands-on time: 1 hour

Total time: 5 hours 30 minutes

For the praline paste

100g whole hazelnuts

25g granulated sugar

For the praline crème mousseline

250ml whole milk

3 egg yolks

70g caster sugar

35g cornflour

125g praline paste (see above)

125g butter

1. First, make the praline paste. Preheat the oven to 180°C, and spread the nuts out on a baking tray. Roast for 10–15 minutes, until you can smell them. Remove from the oven and, if your hazelnuts have skins on them, rub them in a tea towel to remove the skins. Pulse the skinned, roasted nuts in a food processor with the sugar until the nuts release their oils and turn into a paste: you may need to stop the processor and scrape down the sides a few times to encourage the nuts to form a paste, but persevere, it will happen.

2. To make the mousseline, heat the milk to steaming in a saucepan over a medium heat. Whisk together the egg yolks and sugar until they are pale, then whisk in the cornflour. When the milk is steaming, stream a third of it into the egg yolk mixture, whisking to combine, then pour all the mixture into the pan. Bring up to the boil, whisking the whole time – you should see big volcanic bubbles coming up. Stir through the praline paste, then remove from the heat and immediately whisk the butter into the mix: it will melt, keep stirring it until the mixture is smooth. Decant the mousseline into a bowl, cover with clingfilm so that it touches the surface, cool and refrigerate for at least 4 hours, or overnight.

For the craquelin

100g plain flour

100g demerara sugar

100g butter

For the choux

50g butter

½ teaspoon salt

1 tablespoon caster sugar

120ml whole milk

75g strong white bread flour

3 eggs, beaten

3. Beat together all the craquelin ingredients until they form a smooth dough. Roll this out between two pieces of baking paper until they are 2mm thick. Freeze for at least 20 minutes.

4. Once the craquelin dough is very firm, stamp four 8cm circles out of the dough, and then stamp 3cm circles right in the centres, so that you end up with rings of craquelin. You can return these to the freezer until you're ready to use them.

5. Heat the oven to 200°C. Make the choux. Heat the butter, salt, sugar and milk together in a large saucepan over a medium-high heat until the milk reaches the boil. Add the flour in one go and stir rapidly into the liquid to form a dough. Cook over the stove, stirring, until the dough comes away from the sides of the pan and you can hear it sizzle; this should only take a couple of minutes. Turn the dough out on to a large dinner plate and leave to cool for around 10 minutes, until the dough is warm, rather than hot.

6. Once slightly cooled, place the mixture in a bowl and add the beaten eggs in small increments, beating each addition thoroughly into the mixture. You will probably only need 2 of the eggs, so go slowly. When you think the choux is ready, pick up a dollop of the batter on your spatula and shake it off: if what remains on the spatula drops down in a deep 'V' shape, you have added enough egg; if not, add a little more and test again.

7. Draw four 8cm rings on a sheet of baking paper, and then in the centre of each one, draw a 3cm ring (I draw round biscuit cutters). Turn the baking paper upside down – or you'll end up with biro on your choux pastry – on to a large baking tray. Spoon the choux into a piping bag fitted with a medium-sized star piping nozzle. Using your marks as a guide, pipe rings of choux pastry on to the baking paper. Place one of your craquelin rings directly on top of each of your piped choux rings.

8. Bake for 15 minutes, then drop the oven temperature to 160°C. Bake for another 10 minutes, then open the oven to release any built-up steam, and bake for a final 5 minutes. The choux is ready when it releases from the paper-lined tray, and moves around easily. Pierce the base of each round twice with a slim skewer to release any steam. Set to one side on a cooling rack.

9. Once cool, slice each of the Paris-Brests in half horizontally using a serrated knife. Whisk the mousseline until it is thick and smooth; decant into a piping bag. I use an 11mm star nozzle to pipe the mousseline, but it's not essential. Pipe generous amounts of mousseline all the way round the bottom half of each choux ring, then put the top halves back on top. Serve straight away.

St Louis gooey butter cake

Like all the best dishes, St Louis gooey butter cake is said to have been born from a kitchen disaster. The story goes that it was created after a baker mixed up the proportions for a cake, but as it happened during the Great Depression, he baked it off, sliced it up and sold it – and it was a colossal hit.

While stories such as this are normally little more than PR, it almost feels implausible that this cake could have been planned: two separate layers, one a buttery almost biscuity dough, and then on top of that a sweet, gooey puddle which is custardy in texture but caramel in flavour.

The key to this cake is not to overcook it; it is ready when the outer edge of the crust is firm, but the very centre still has a jaunty jiggle.

Makes: 16 squares

Hands-on time: 20 minutes

Total time: 3–4 hours

For the base

30ml whole milk

1 teaspoon dried, instant yeast

45g butter, soft

15g caster sugar

½ teaspoon fine salt

1 egg

135g plain flour

For the topping

90g butter, soft

150g caster sugar

½ teaspoon vanilla paste

½ teaspoon fine salt

1 egg

30g golden syrup

2 tablespoons water

100g plain flour

15g cornflour

icing sugar, to dust

1. Make the base. Heat the milk in a small pan until just above blood temperature: if you dip your finger into the milk it should just feel warm. Sprinkle the yeast into the milk, and stir to combine.

2. In a stand mixer, cream together the butter, sugar and salt until pale and fluffy, then add the egg, making sure it is fully combined. Fold in the flour, then stir through the yeast and milk mixture. Beat with the paddle attachment for 7 minutes, until the dough pulls away from the sides of the bowl.

3. Butter a 20 x 20cm square cake tin and press the dough into it with your fingers, nudging it into an even layer that spreads to each side and the corners. The dough will be quite sticky, so I find it easiest to do this with slightly damp fingers. Cover with clingfilm or a clean tea towel, and leave to rise in a warm place for 2–3 hours.

4. The dough won't look terribly risen when it's had its time, but it should no longer be sticky, and will feel a bit puffy. When the bottom layer is risen, preheat the oven to 170°C. Cream together the butter, sugar, vanilla paste and salt for the topping until pale and fluffy. Beat in the egg until completely combined. Loosen the golden syrup with the 2 tablespoons of water and add that to the mix, followed by the flour and cornflour.

5. Dollop the topping on to the risen dough, gently smoothing it into an even layer. Bake for 20–25 minutes. It will still be liquid in the centre. Allow to cool completely before dusting with icing sugar and slicing straight from the tin.

Makes: 12 doughnuts

Hands-on time: 1 hour

Total time: 5 hours

For the doughnuts

400g strong white bread flour

2 teaspoons dried, instant yeast

30g caster sugar

1 teaspoon fine salt

200ml whole milk

2 eggs

80g butter, soft

vegetable oil, for deep-frying

For the vanilla custard

250ml whole milk

1 teaspoon vanilla paste

3 egg yolks

40g caster sugar

20g cornflour

100ml double cream

For the rhubarb and vanilla jam

200g rhubarb, chopped

1 vanilla pod, halved and seeds removed

200g granulated sugar

1 tablespoon lemon juice

To coat

caster sugar

1. Mix all the doughnut ingredients apart from the butter and oil together in a stand mixer with a dough hook attachment. Knead the dough until it is smooth and supple (this should take about 5 minutes).

2. Add the butter to the dough in five separate additions, kneading each in well before adding the next. Place the dough in a clean bowl, cover it with clingfilm, and leave to rise until doubled in size, about 2 hours.

3. Meanwhile, you can make the fillings: to make the vanilla custard, heat the milk and vanilla paste to steaming in a medium-sized pan over a medium heat. Whisk the egg yolks and sugar together in a heatproof bowl until pale and thick, then whisk in the cornflour. Stream some of the hot milk into the egg yolks, whisking the whole time. Pour the milk-loosened egg mixture into the pan, and cook over a medium heat, whisking constantly. It will become very thick; keep cooking and whisking until the mixture boils, then remove from the heat, decant on to a plate, cover with clingfilm (the clingfilm should touch the surface of the custard to stop a skin forming), and leave to cool completely.

4. To make the jam, place the rhubarb, vanilla pod and seeds, and sugar in a large heavy-based saucepan and heat very gently until the sugar has dissolved. Then increase the heat and cook, stirring continuously, until the mixture reaches 105°C. Set to one side to cool; you can remove the vanilla pod, and give the jam a spritz of lemon juice.

5. Punch down the risen dough to get rid of the build-up of gas, turn it out on to an unfloured surface, and divide it into 60g portions.

6. Take one portion of dough and flatten it with the palm of your hand. Now fold all the edges into the centre of the dough, and turn it upside down so the smooth side of the dough is facing upright. Make your hand into a cage shape, place this over the dough and, with the tips of your fingers touching the work surface, make small circular motions around the dough: you can exert a little bit of squashy pressure on the dough here. This friction will force the seams under the dough and, when you remove your hand, a perfect little smooth ball should spring up. Try to avoid flouring your dough, as you need the friction from the work surface. Transfer to a lightly oiled tray or board, and repeat with the remaining dough portions. Space the dough balls well apart, cover lightly with oiled clingfilm, and leave to prove for 2 hours, or until doubled in size.

7. When the doughnuts are ready to fry, they will be airy and puffy and visibly larger than before. It will take about 15 minutes to heat up your oil: heat a deep-fat fryer or a deep-sided, heavy-based pan with

Brown butter old fashioned

Butter-washing bourbon (page 278) brings a richness and complexity to the booze, and makes a perfect base for any cocktail, but works especially well in an old fashioned. To me, it smells exactly like Werther's Originals, but as you taste it, that caramel sweetness dissipates, and you're left with the flavour of nuts and vanilla and dark fruits.

Makes: one old fashioned

Hands-on time: 2 minutes

Total time: 2 minutes

½ teaspoon demerara sugar

3 dashes of angostura bitters

1 teaspoon water

the biggest ice cube you can muster

60ml butter-washed bourbon (see page 278)

a thick ribbon of orange zest, to garnish

1. Put the sugar, bitters and water into a small tumbler. Mix until the sugar is partly dissolved.

2. Add the ice cube to the glass and stir in the bourbon. Garnish with the orange zest.

Brown butter bourbon pecan sandies

The flavour of the bourbon really shines through in these wonderfully crumbly cookies. When I first made them, I was genuinely shocked at how strong and complex the flavour of the bourbon was, which I'd feared might disappear: the floral and toffee flavours of the whisky come through, figs and dates, but also pear and citrus.

To ensure that your sandies don't collapse, when you strain the butter from your bourbon, melt it and briefly bring it to a simmer so that any liquid boils off. Decant into a heatproof container, and leave to solidify.

Makes: 12 biscuits

Hands-on time: 15 minutes

Total time: 1 hour 30 minutes

140g bourbon butter (see page 278), cooled until solid, but soft

170g caster sugar

55g light soft brown sugar

2 teaspoons vanilla extract

½ teaspoon fine salt

1 egg yolk

125g plain flour

¼ teaspoon bicarbonate of soda

85g pecans, finely chopped

1. Cream together the butter and both sugars until pale and fluffy. Add the vanilla, salt and egg yolk, mixing until combined. Fold through the flour, bicarbonate of soda and pecans, until you have a thick, firm dough.

2. Roll into tablespoon-sized balls, then refrigerate for at least an hour, or overnight.

3. When you're ready to bake, preheat the oven to 180°C, and line two baking trays with baking paper.

4. Space the balls well apart on the trays, and flatten each a little with the base of a glass, so that they sit flat.

5. Bake for 15 minutes, until golden-brown, then leave to cool on the baking trays for 15 minutes before transferring to a cooling rack.

286 Paratha

289 Sour cream and chive butter American biscuits

291 Rough puff pastry

294 Rough puff sausage rolls

296 Puff pastry

298 Piña colada galette des rois

300 Inverse puff pastry

302 Wild mushroom, tarragon and crème fraîche pithivier

305 Blackberry and pistachio mille-feuille

308 Cheese twists

309 Orange and coriander seed palmiers

310 Arlettes

313 Croissants

316 Pains au chocolat

317 Pains au rhum et raisin

318 Blackberry and bay custard Danishes

320 Kouign amann

324 Brioche feuilletée

Rough puff sausage rolls

I could measure my life in sausage rolls: the stalwart of birthdays, Christmases and brownie guide parties of the late 80s and early 90s, to the Gregg's that sustained me through my years at the criminal bar, via the cold, flabby ones from a corner shop that became my go-to after a night on the tiles, I've eaten more than my fair share of sausage rolls. In fact, I'd go so far as to consider myself an authority on the good, the bad and the ugly of sausage rolls. And these are the greatest of the good.

The mango chutney might seem like a strange addition, but it's one of my best kitchen tricks, bringing just the right amount of aromatic sweetness and spice to the pork. Buy a good brand (I use Geeta's) and the hum of ginger and spice, and little jewels of fruit, will bring your sausage rolls to life.

Makes: 12 chunky sausage rolls or 20 party-sized slices

Hands-on time: 20 minutes

Total time: 1 hour 15 minutes

6 pork or Cumberland sausages

1½ tablespoons mango chutney

1 teaspoon English mustard

½ tablespoon Worcestershire sauce

½ teaspoon ground white pepper

300g rough puff pastry (see page 291)

1 egg, beaten, to glaze

2 tablespoons sesame seeds, for sprinkling

1. First, make your sausage mix. Slit each sausage lengthways and peel the skin away, tipping the sausage meat into a bowl. Add the mango chutney, mustard, Worcestershire sauce and white pepper, mixing together thoroughly.

2. Roll the puff pastry into a rectangle, measuring approximately 35 x 25cm, trim the edges to straighten, and cut in half horizontally.

3. You should now have two long strips of pastry. Transfer each of these to a large baking paper-lined baking tray, and place a line of sausage meat along the middle of each strip. To fit it on, I tend to arrange my pastry strip on the diagonal along the baking tray. If you don't have one that will fit the whole thing, you can cut the pastry in half across the middle, and have two sausage rolls on one tray.

4. Paint the edge of the pastry nearest to you with the beaten egg. Fold the edge of the pastry furthest away from you over the sausage meat so that it meets the egg wash and sticks. Using the back of a fork, press the pastry where it meets all the way along the strip. Paint the entire strip with the egg wash, and sprinkle with sesame seeds. Refrigerate for 30 minutes.

5. Preheat the oven to 200°C. Bake the pastry for 25 minutes, until the pastry is golden and puffed. Using a bread knife, carefully (use a sawing action, rather than a down-cutting action), slice the cooked sausage rolls into 12 chunky sausage rolls, or 20 party-sized slices.

Serves: 4

Hands-on time: 30 minutes

Total time: 3 hours 20 minutes

20g dried porcini mushrooms

150g oyster mushrooms

250g chestnut mushrooms

15g butter

1 tablespoon cider or white wine vinegar

3 tablespoons crème fraîche

1 tablespoon shredded fresh tarragon

½ teaspoon fine salt

freshly ground black pepper

300g puff or inverse puff pastry (see pages 296 and 300)

1 egg yolk, beaten, to glaze

1. First, cover the dried porcini mushrooms in boiling water, and leave to soak while you cook the other mushrooms.

2. While the porcini are soaking, halve the oyster mushrooms and slice them, and slice the chestnut mushrooms. Heat a heavy-based frying pan over a medium-high heat and melt the butter in it. Sauté the oyster mushrooms until golden-brown, add the vinegar, let it cook off, then set the mushrooms to one side. Cook the chestnut mushrooms in the same pan until they have given up their water and begun to sizzle.

3. Drain and roughly chop the rehydrated porcini mushrooms. Combine the porcini, oyster, and chestnut mushrooms, along with the crème fraîche and the tarragon, and season generously with the salt and some pepper. Line a bowl approximately 15cm across with clingfilm, spoon the creamy mushroom mixture into it, pack it down into an even layer (don't worry, it won't fill the bowl) and freeze for an hour until firm.

4. Meanwhile, roll out the puff pastry to the thickness of a pound coin. Later, you're going to need to cut one 20cm and one 23cm disc from the pastry, so check that your rolled pastry is big enough to accommodate this. Divide the pastry in half, then transfer the two sheets of pastry on to a chopping board or tray with a sheet of baking paper between them. Refrigerate for at least 30 minutes.

5. Cut out two discs, one 23cm, one 20cm, from the chilled pastry. Place the smaller disc on a baking paper-lined baking tray. Turn the chilled mushroom mixture out on to the centre of the pastry, removing the clingfilm from it, and dab a border of water around the edge of the pastry. Lay the second, larger disc on top. Smooth the top layer of pastry down over the mixture, to reduce air bubbles, and press the edges down with the tines of a fork to seal. Paint all over with egg yolk, and refrigerate for 20 minutes.

6. Preheat the oven to 200°C. Paint the pastry with another coat of egg yolk and then, using the back of a small knife, make swooping marks from the centre of the pastry down towards the edge. Prick a hole in the centre, to act as a vent. Bake for 15 minutes, then drop the temperature to 170°C and bake for another 45 minutes until puffed and golden. Serve hot.

Blackberry and pistachio mille-feuille

Mille-feuille translates as 'a thousand leaves' and refers to the many layers of flaky puff pastry within one of these French custard slices. It can be unwieldy to eat or (whisper it) annoyingly inelegant and top-heavy for a pastry which requires a lot of time and precision. My way around this is using caramelised puff pastry.

Caramelised puff pastry is a neat technique; it improves the texture and flavour of an already brilliant foodstuff, and makes it easier to eat. It ensures thin, crisp, ridiculously flaky pastry, which is sweet and a little caramelised. To make this, you follow the normal method for making puff, but then you dust it with icing sugar, and bake it under a heavy baking tray. This weight prevents the puff from rising like it usually would, keeping the layers tightly close to one another. When it's baked, it is golden-brown with beautiful distinct layers – it's like minimalist puff pastry.

Layered up with fruit and cream between those even layers of delicate pastry, it's a total joy to eat. The slight fruity tartness of the blackberries alongside the buttery, sweet pistachios is a perfect match. And it's pretty visually satisfying: the glimpse of those little blackberries, sitting up proudly on their bums, blue-black, alongside the bright, exciting jade green pistachio cream.

I've used unsweetened pistachio paste here: if yours has sugar or sweeteners in it, hold off adding the icing sugar until you have stirred the paste into the cream, then taste it, and decide whether you want to add further sweetness.

Makes: 6 mille-feuilles

Hands-on time: 30 minutes

Total time: 1 hour 30 minutes

6 tablespoons icing sugar,
plus extra for dusting

300g puff pastry

250g small fresh blackberries

For the pistachio cream

100g unsweetened pistachio
paste

300ml double cream

50g icing sugar

½ teaspoon vanilla paste

1. Line an upside-down baking tray with baking paper, and sift 3 tablespoons of the icing sugar evenly across the paper.

2. On a lightly floured surface, roll out the puff pastry to a square measuring 35 x 35cm. Lay the pastry on top of the icing-sugared baking paper, and sift the remaining 3 tablespoons of icing sugar across the top of the pastry. Cover with a second sheet of baking paper, and put into the freezer for 30 minutes.

3. Preheat the oven to 200°C. Remove the tray from the freezer and place another baking tray on top, this time the right way up. If your tray isn't terribly heavy (mine isn't), place an ovenproof saucepan on top to weigh it down and keep the pastry from rising. Bake for 25-30 minutes, until the pastry is golden-brown and crisp all over.

4. Remove the saucepan, if using (careful, the handle will be red hot!), the top tray, and the top sheet of baking paper, and transfer the puff pastry on its bottom sheet of baking paper on to a cooling rack.

5. Once the puff pastry is cool, using a bread knife, straighten up the edges: go slowly and use a gentle sawing action, rather than a cutting down motion, and you should be able to get really neat lines. Cut the rectangle into 18 rectangles measuring 5 x 10cm each.

6. Make the pistachio cream. Place the pistachio paste, cream, icing sugar and vanilla in a large bowl. Whisk gently to break up the pistachio paste. Whisk with more energy to bring to medium peaks, so that the cream holds its own weight. Transfer into a piping bag fitted with a star nozzle, and refrigerate until you're ready to use it.

7. To assemble your mille-feuilles, place one of your pieces of puff pastry on a flat surface. Pipe a blob of pistachio cream in one corner of the pastry, and place a blackberry next to it. Continue alternating pistachio cream and blackberries until you have covered the surface of the pastry. Place another layer of puff pastry on top, and repeat with the pistachio cream and blackberries. Top with a final layer of puff pastry. Dust with icing sugar, and serve.

TAKE A TABLESPOON OF BUTTER. . .

There are all sorts of recipes in this book where butter is the star of the show: kouign amann, croissants, brioche, beurre blanc, proper mashed potato.

But there's also a host of dishes – barely recipes – where butter is more of a support act. That's not to underplay it; butter can make an enormous difference to so many dishes that don't technically require it in the recipe. It can bring richness, creaminess, gloss and shine, and a small amount can make a big difference. Try the following to enrich and enhance your cooking.

- Add 2 tablespoons of butter to your standard brown bread recipe just before you start kneading it and find out how much it lifts the loaf – creating a softer crumb, and a lighter flavour.

- A tablespoon of butter dotted on to the top of an oven-baked rice pudding before it bakes gives it a better skin: burnished, glossy, thick. Just like a proper old-fashioned rice pudding should be.

- A tablespoon of butter stirred into a still warm ganache, before it sets, will give you a more rounded flavour and a slightly firmer set – making it perfect for piping.

- Whisk 2 tablespoons of butter into a batch of warm crème pâtissière, then let it cool and whisk, for an impossibly silky texture.

- Stir a tablespoon of butter into hot porridge for a gently rich and creamy breakfast – try using the date and cardamom butter, the orange and ginger butter, or the brandy butter (see pages 34–35).

- A tablespoon of butter sitting on a pile of steaming vegetables is a beautiful thing, intensifying their colour and flavour.

- Roast fruit (quince, rhubarb, apples, pears, plums, peaches, apricots, pineapple or figs) with a generous knob of butter, and a sprinkling of sugar until tender: this will soften recalcitrant hard fruit, or breathe second life into fruit that has seen better days. You can add a splash of booze, a crumble of amaretti biscuits, or a sprinkling of orange blossom or rose water.

- Adding a tablespoon of butter to jam or marmalade just as you finish the cooking process will disperse any scum that has risen to the top of the jam as the conserve has boiled. A nifty trick.

Remember that if you're adding butter to a dish that doesn't obviously or conventionally have butter in it, it changes the allergens and dietary requirements in that dish.

332 Bananas Foster

334 Chaussons aux pommes (apple turnovers)

337 Buckwheat galettes with butter-fried apples
and Calvados ice cream

341 Sticky date and fig pudding

343 Pineapple upside-down tarte Tatin

344 Marmalade and dark chocolate bread and
butter pudding

345 Clementine Sussex pond pudding

349 Damson plum crumble

350 Christmas cake

352 Christmas pudding

357 Boxing Day Christmas pudding fried in butter

Chaussons aux pommes
(apple turnovers)

When we were little, we used to go on holiday to a small village in Brittany. There was a street stall that only sold apples encased in pastry. It was a roving stall, but I remember being told that there was a new batch coming, and waiting on the street for them to emerge, sweet and flaky, still crackling from the oven; the innards sweet–sour, soft and yielding and volcanically hot.

Apple turnovers as they're known in the UK, or chaussons aux pommes (apple slippers) in French, are just puff pastry enclosing an apple compote; by rights, they shouldn't be as good as they are, but then tart apples and rich, flaky pastry have always been happy bedfellows: the French legend of their origin comes from 1630, when the people of Saint Calais were suffering an epidemic, and starving for lack of food. The local châtelaine distributed flour and apples to the poor, and they made chaussons aux pommes.

They are perfect with ice cream, but my shameful secret is that I like them with squirty cream from a can.

It's no surprise that other fruits are just as beautiful encased in sugar-dotted puff pastry. My favourites are quince, or rhubarb. Take 2 quince, and peel, quarter and core them. Omit the cinnamon and replace with ½ a star anise, add 30g of caster sugar, cover with water and poach gently for an hour until softened (quince will never collapse quite like apples will), drain and cool and follow the recipe overleaf from step 3. For rhubarb, simmer 300g of chopped rhubarb with 2 tablespoons of caster sugar until softened but not yet a purée; strain in a sieve to drain off excess liquid, then follow the recipe from step 3.

Makes: 6 apple turnovers

Hands-on time: 20 minutes

Total time: 1 hour 20 minutes

2 tart eating apples, peeled, cored and cut into small dice

25g light soft brown sugar

¼ teaspoon ground cinnamon

1 tablespoon lemon juice

2 tablespoons water

400g puff pastry (see page 296)

50g caster sugar

50ml water

2 tablespoons demerara sugar (optional)

1. Make the apple filling. Cook the apples, brown sugar, cinnamon, lemon juice and water together in a small pan for 10 minutes, until the apple is soft and luscious, but not without texture. Set aside to cool completely.

2. Meanwhile, roll out the puff pastry into 2 sheets about the thickness of a pound coin, place on baking paper-lined baking trays, and refrigerate for 30 minutes.

3. Preheat the oven to 200°C. Cut six 12cm discs from the chilled puff pastry, and remove the excess pastry. Divide the filling between the discs, spooning it right into the centre. Dab the edges of each disc with water, then pull one side of the pastry over on to the other, and press gently to seal, to create a semi-circular filled pastry. Make three small cuts in the centre of each pastry to act as vents for the steam.

4. Bake for 15 minutes, then lower the temperature to 170°C and bake for another 15 minutes, until golden and puffed.

5. While the pastries are baking, make a simple syrup from the caster sugar and water: place in a small pan, given them a quick stir together, then bring up to a simmer. Set to one side.

6. Glaze the chaussons with the syrup, sprinkle with the demerara sugar if using, and return to the oven for just a couple of minutes. Enjoy these apple pies warm, but as anyone who has ever eaten a McDonald's apple pie knows, when first cooked, they will be volcanically hot.

Pineapple upside-down tarte Tatin

Pineapple upside-down tarte Tatin is a bit of a tautology: a tarte Tatin is necessarily cooked upside down, the fruit caramelising against the base of the pan, the puff pastry sitting on top, before the whole thing is bravely flipped on to a serving plate. In a sense, tarte Tatin is the choicest of upside-down cakes. But a tarte Tatin is traditionally apple, occasionally pear or apricot.

Here the pineapple and cherries are arranged in the bottom of the pan like in the retro upside-down cake, thick rings of pineapple, dotted with bright glacé fruit. Caramelised pineapple is a particular joy. The sugars in the fruit take very well to heat and the application of a bit of butter and sugar, which makes them perfect for a pudding like this.

Makes: enough for 6

Hands-on time: 15 minutes

Total time: 1 hour 20 minutes

350g puff pastry

70g caster sugar

50g salted butter

1 teaspoon vanilla paste

7 canned pineapple rings

19 glacé cherries (morello, if you can get them)

1. Roll out the puff pastry on a lightly floured surface to 0.5cm thick and cut out a 30cm circle, using a dinner plate as a guide. Place the disc on a baking sheet or chopping board, lightly prick all over with a fork, and refrigerate for 30 minutes.

2. Preheat the oven to 200°C. Place the caster sugar in a heavy-based, ovenproof frying pan, measuring approximately 20cm across. Cook over a medium heat until the sugar melts and forms an amber caramel. As soon as it starts to smoke, remove from the heat and whisk in the butter, followed by the vanilla paste.

3. Carefully lay out the pineapple rings directly on to the caramel, placing them as close to one another as possible. Place a glacé cherry in each gap.

4. Lay the chilled puff over the top of the fruit, easing the edges of the pastry down so that they curve round into the pan. Using a sharp knife, prick a couple of vents in the middle of the pastry. Place in the oven, immediately drop the temperature to 180°C, and bake for 30 minutes.

5. Remove from the oven (be careful as the handle will be hot!). Leave to cool for 5 minutes. Gently twist the pastry to release the caramel from the pan. Remembering that the handle of the pan will still be really hot, place a large serving plate directly over the pastry, and swiftly invert. If you accidentally leave the pudding for too long and the caramel sets, making it impossible to turn out, simply flash the pan briefly over a flame on the hob, or pop it into a low oven for a couple of minutes: the caramel will soften and release.

Marmalade and dark chocolate bread and butter pudding

My mother was not a pudding-maker. The exception was her bread and butter pudding, which would sit in the bottom of a low oven after the roast was served. It was spread with pineapple jam, and the egg custard was whisked to billy-o, so it would balloon up in the oven like a soufflé. Mine is a little different, but it occupies the same place in our lives: it is a big, proud pudding, made to be brought out after a Sunday lunch.

Unlike the bread and butter puddings I grew up with – sliced white loaves, buttered then sliced – the butter here is found in the brioche and the custard. The brioche should be very thickly sliced, and left to sit in the custard, so it can absorb as much of it as possible. The more of that gorgeous custard that the beautiful brioche can suck up, the more luscious the pudding will be.

The slight bitterness of the marmalade and the dark chocolate dotted throughout cuts through the custard, and makes something extravagant and indulgent dangerously easy to eat. My favourite kind of pudding.

Makes: enough for 8

Hands-on time: 15 minutes

Total time: 1 hour 10 minutes

400g brioche

300ml whole milk

200ml double cream

50g butter

½ teaspoon vanilla paste

4 eggs

3 tablespoons caster sugar

75g dark chocolate, roughly chopped

150g Seville orange marmalade

1 tablespoon demerara sugar

1. Preheat the oven to 150°C. Cut the brioche into thick slices, then halve them on the diagonal into triangles.

2. Heat the milk and cream together with the butter and vanilla paste in a saucepan over a medium heat, until it starts to simmer. Whisk the eggs and caster sugar together in a large, heatproof bowl, and pour the hot milk and cream over the top, whisking the whole time.

3. Place the brioche slices in the custard mixture, and leave to absorb the mixture for 10 minutes.

4. After the soaking time, place half the soaked brioche in a large (I use an enamel rectangular dish, measuring 15 x 25cm, but it's not a precise art) ovenproof dish. Dot half the dark chocolate across the bread, and little puddles of marmalade. Place the second half of the soaked bread on top, pour over the remaining custard, and dot with the rest of the chocolate and marmalade. Sprinkle with the demerara sugar.

5. Bake for 45 minutes, until puffed, golden, and still a little wibbly when you jostle the dish.

Clementine Sussex pond pudding

Given that this book is called 'Butter', it's perhaps unsurprising that we haven't seen a lot of suet up to this point. Suet and butter tend to be an either/or situation – often, both will do the same job equally well, but you plump for one rather than the other. Here, the role of butter is not in the pastry, but in the filling, which means that butter can sit alongside suet.

A Sussex pond pudding is full of butter; at one point it was known as a 'butter pond pudding' – and the citrus element, the gorgeous surprise in the centre, is relatively new. The first recorded recipe for the pudding describes it as a piece of pastry wrapped around a 'great piece of Butter'. It wasn't until Jane Grigson's recipe in *English Food* in 1974 that the Sussex pond pudding began habitually to include a lemon.

I agree with Grigson that the inclusion of citrus is essential: that contrast of bitter and sour with the rich, sweet butter sauce is the joy of the dish, but the thin-skinned clementine is a delightful alternative to the now traditional lemon. As they steam, the clementines almost candy inside, bathed in the spiced melted butter and sugar sauce, and the pastry is suffused with butter and infused with the fragrant spiced clementine.

The pudding should stand proudly when turned out, but will collapse when cut into, giving up its spiced citrus – and the combination of spectacle and spiced clementine make this a beautiful alternative to a Christmas pudding.

Serves: 4

Hands-on time: 20 minutes

Total time: 3 hours 20 minutes

200g self-raising flour,
plus extra for dusting

100g shredded suet

½ teaspoon fine salt

125ml whole milk

100g butter, cut into small dice,
plus extra for greasing

100g light soft brown sugar

½ teaspoon ground mixed spice

2 clementines

1. First, generously grease a 600ml pudding basin (approx. 16cm diameter) with butter, and put a full kettle on to boil.

2. Whisk together the self-raising flour, suet, and salt in a bowl. Add the milk and bring it together into a dough, first with a knife, then, as the mixture becomes more cohesive, with your hands.

3. Reserve a quarter of the pastry for the lid, and roll out the rest using a floured rolling pin to make a large circle. Ease this into the greased pudding basin and smooth it so it is flush against the side of the pudding basin.

4. Toss the diced butter, sugar and mixed spice together in a bowl, and place a layer in the bottom of the pastry-lined basin.

5. Prick the clementines all over with a sharp skewer. Place them in the pudding basin, side by side, and fill the rest of the cavity with the remaining spiced butter and sugar. Roll the reserved pastry into a 16cm circle, for the lid. Wet the edges of the pastry case with a little water, then place the lid on top, pressing gently to seal.

6. To prepare the pudding basin, place a piece of baking paper on top of a piece of tin foil, and fold both along the middle to create a pleat (this is so when the pudding expands, it doesn't burst out of the paper). Place these two folded sheets over the top of the pudding basin, centring the pleat. Tie tightly with string. Alternatively, if you have heat-safe clingfilm, you can place a pleated disc of baking paper over the top of the pudding basin, and wrap the whole pudding basin twice-round in heat-safe clingfilm.

7. To steam, place a clean tea towel in the base of a large saucepan. Fill the pan halfway up with boiling water. Lower the prepared pudding into the pan: the water should come about two-thirds of the way up the pudding basin. Put the pan over a very low heat and cover with a lid. Steam for 3 hours. Keep an eye on the water level, checking every 30 minutes or so: it is dangerous for the pan to boil dry, so top up with boiling water from the kettle, if needed.

8. To serve, lift the basin carefully from the pan of water, and remove the wrappings and any string. Run a knife around the edge of the basin, being careful not to cut into the pastry. Place a serving plate over the top of the pudding, and swiftly invert.

Damson plum crumble

I love crumble. I mean I *really, really* love crumble. Like pizza, heist movies, and advent calendars, even a 'bad' crumble is actually pretty good.

But a truly excellent crumble can be difficult to come by. If I'm making a crumble, I don't want to end up with a cobbler, but I also don't want the topping to go too far the other way, and end up with something dusty and mealy. Happily, there are two easy fixes. The first is a good proportion of butter. The second is a nifty little trick I borrow from Nigel Slater: a few drops of water sprinkled over the crumble mix bind the mixture just enough so that as it cooks, it will be crunchy on the top, soft beneath; perfect.

Makes: enough for 6

Hands-on time: 15 minutes

Total time: 1 hour 15 minutes

For the fruit

600g fresh damsons (unstoned weight)

50ml water

2 large eating apples

1 tablespoon light soft brown sugar (optional)

For the crumble

100g salted butter, cold

125g plain flour

60g light soft brown sugar

½ teaspoon ground cardamom

30g oats

30g chopped hazelnuts (optional)

1 tablespoon demerara sugar

1. Prepare the fruit. Place the stoned damsons in a pan with 50ml of water, and cook over a low heat until the damsons soften, about 10 minutes. Remove from the heat, and leave until cool enough to handle.

2. Once the damsons are no longer scalding, you can squidge them with your hands to release the stones. Discard the stones (be vigilant, they're small and slippery) and drain off any liquid that has collected. Taste the soft damsons; you may wish to add the brown sugar, depending on their sweetness.

3. Preheat the oven to 200°C. Peel and core the apples, and cut them into slices about 2.5cm thick. Put them in the bottom of a large ovenproof dish, add the stewed damsons and gently mix together.

4. Make the crumble. In a large bowl, rub the butter into the flour using your fingertips, until it resembles breadcrumbs. Stir the brown sugar through the mix, followed by the cardamom, oats and hazelnuts, if using. Drizzle a tablespoon of water into the mixture and stir until some of the mixture slightly clumps together.

5. Spoon the crumble topping evenly over the fruit, and sprinkle the demerara sugar over the top.

6. Bake for 35 minutes, until the topping is golden and the fruit is bubbling up at the edges. Allow to cool for 10 minutes, then serve with custard or thick cream.

Christmas cake

I don't really have a recipe inheritance. There are a few scant dishes that I have in my mother's or granny's handwriting, or that I've reverse-engineered in the years since they died (my mother's pasta bake, and her vol-au-vents fillings; my paternal grandmother's date and walnut cake). I am, as a consequence, obsessed with the idea of recipes being passed down between family and friends, with traditions established, disrupted and mutated, with how those recipes change in different hands and what they represent.

One of the recipes I do have is for a light fruit cake, made with canned pineapple.

It is hard to overestimate the importance of fruit cake in my house. I know, I know, it sounds like I'm exaggerating, but I'm not. My husband and his family are obsessed with the stuff: so common was it in the Palin household that Sam grew up believing that, in the same way when we say 'Christmas cake' we mean 'fruit cake', 'birthday cake' was of the same ilk. On our first date, knowing how important fruit cake was to Sam, I took him a loaf of that pineapple fruit cake.

After I'd demonstrated my commitment to Sam, I was inducted into the secrets of the Palin family fruit cake recipe, but because I am an ingrate and can't resist a recipe fiddle, I played around with it. It is based on the blueprint of the Palin fruit cake, but also boasts puréed pineapple as a nod to Mum's cake, which bring tartness and uniform moistness to the cake. I suppose, in a way, it's a marriage of two families' beloved cakes.

This makes a very deep 20cm fruit cake: the raw mixture will come right to the top of the tin, but don't worry, it barely rises at all. I then feed it whenever I remember (every week or fortnight) for the following six months, before icing it with a thick layer of marzipan and then fondant icing. In this state, sozzled, sugar-drunk, and packed with dried fruit, it will keep virtually indefinitely.

Makes: one 20cm fruit cake (serves 12)

Hands-on time: 20 minutes

Total time: 3 hours 20 minutes

225g butter

225g dark muscovado sugar

1 tablespoon black treacle

340g plain flour

2 teaspoons ground cinnamon

2 teaspoons ground mixed spice

½ teaspoon salt

4 eggs

4 tablespoons rum

100g dried morello cherries (glacé cherries are fine)

1kg mixed dried fruit

4 balls of stem ginger in syrup, drained and finely chopped

1 x 227g can pineapple, drained

100g whole skin-on almonds, roughly chopped

1 lemon, finely zested

1 clementine, finely zested

1. First, line your tin. Because this is going to bake for so long, it needs more lining than most cakes: grease the base and sides of your deep, 20cm round cake tin, and line with two layers of baking paper, making sure the paper at the sides extends higher than the top of the tin. Wrap the outside of the cake tin with two layers of brown paper or baking paper around the sides and tie with ovenproof string, again making sure the paper extends up higher than the top of the tin. Preheat the oven to 150°C.

2. Cream together the butter, sugar and treacle in a bowl until the mixture has lightened in colour and texture.

3. In a separate bowl, sift together the flour, cinnamon, mixed spice and salt, and whisk together the eggs and rum in a jug. Alternately add the flour and egg mixtures to the creamed butter and sugar, stirring thoroughly after each addition.

4. Stir in all the dried fruit, ginger, pineapple, nuts, and both zests.

5. Spoon into your prepared tin, level the top, and place another disc of baking paper on top: this will stop the cake doming too much.

6. Bake for about 3 hours, until a cocktail stick inserted into the cake comes out clean; cover with tin foil if the top starts to look very brown – check for this after the 2-hour mark. Once cooked, leave the cake to cool completely in the tin, before removing the baking paper. You can decorate your cake with thick marzipan and fondant or snow-white royal icing, or cover the top with apricot jam and mixed nuts and candied fruit, gleaming and jewel-like.

Christmas pudding

I used to be ambivalent about Christmas puddings; I didn't really understand their appeal, and I definitely had never made one of my own. But Kate was their biggest fan, and used to tell me about making them to her great-granny's recipe in Australia, boiling them in cloth, and hanging them in airing cupboards until they dried out.

Kate's enthusiasm for the pudding was so infectious, that I found myself standing next to her over an enormous plastic storage tub, in which sat dozens of eggs, kilos of butter, and more dried fruit than I'd ever seen in my life. Kate opened the first of several bottles of booze and poured the whole thing into the dark, sticky mix.

As I wobbled home with two extremely large and one regular-sized Christmas puddings, ready to commit a day of my life to steaming them, I thought it was probably time I learnt to love the pud.

It turns out I had nothing to worry about. Where I'd only previously had the shop-bought versions, that were dark and currant-laden, a little stodgy and one-note, a proper homemade Christmas pudding was an entirely different beast: sweet and surprisingly light, packed with plump moist fruits (and veg!), and fragrant and complex. I was an immediate convert.

So this recipe is based on Kate's (and her great-granny's), although with some fiddling from me: I've added stout or porter, for those malty, treacly tones, and prunes, figs and dates join the other dried fruits, to bring sticky, toffee, chewiness to the proceedings – and I make mine not in the bowling ball shape, but in a pudding-shape, as I find them easier to store.

Makes: one 1kg pudding, serving 6–8 (recipe easily doubled, or tripled)

Hands-on time: 30 minutes

Total time: 7 hours

75g prunes, chopped

80g soft dried figs, chopped

50g glacé cherries, halved

75g dates, stoned and chopped

100g mixed dried fruit

1 small eating apple, cored and grated

1 small carrot, peeled and grated

2 tablespoons bitter orange marmalade

½ teaspoon ground nutmeg

½ teaspoon ground cinnamon

1 tablespoon ground mixed spice

1 tablespoon golden syrup

75ml stout or porter

115g butter, soft

115g light soft brown sugar

2 eggs

55g self-raising flour

55g plain flour

½ teaspoon salt

65g fresh breadcrumbs

40g flaked almonds

50ml whisky

1. Mix all your dried fruits, grated apple and carrot, marmalade, spices and golden syrup together with the stout or porter in a saucepan, stir, bring to the boil, turn off the heat, and leave for an hour.

2. In a bowl, cream together the butter and sugar until pale brown and fluffy in texture. Add the eggs, one at a time, completely combining with the mixture before adding the next. Stir through both flours, the salt and breadcrumbs. Stir in the flaked almonds, soaked fruit, any residual stout or porter, and the whisky until combined. Spoon the mixture into a 20cm pudding basin.

3. Place a piece of baking paper on top of a piece of tin foil, and fold both along the middle to create a pleat (this is so when the pudding expands, it doesn't burst out of the paper). Place these two folded sheets over the top of the pudding basin, centring the pleat. Tie tightly with string. Alternatively, if you have heat-safe clingfilm, you can place a pleated disc of baking paper over the top of the pudding basin, and wrap the whole pudding basin twice-round in heat-safe clingfilm.

4. To steam, place a clean tea towel in the base of a large saucepan. Fill the pan halfway up with boiling water. Lower the prepared pudding into the pan: the water should come about two-thirds of the way up the pudding basin. Put the pan over a very low heat, and cover the pan with a lid. Steam for 3 hours. Keep an eye on the water level, checking every 30 minutes or so: it is dangerous for the pan to boil dry, so top up with boiling water from the kettle, if needed.

5. When your pudding is cooked, carefully remove it from the pan, remove the tin foil and baking paper and leave the top off the pudding to cool and dry out. Once dry and cool, place a new, clean covering of baking paper and tin foil in the same way as before, and store the pudding in a cool, dry place.

6. When you're ready to eat, steam the pudding in the same manner for 2½ hours. Once the time is up, remove the covering and run a knife round the edge of the basin: the pudding should slip right out. Serve with brandy butter, thick brandy cream, brandy sauce, or ice cream.

buttermilk pancakes 183
jalapeño cornbread with honey butter 177
treacle soda bread 186
butterscotch 207

C

cabbage: colcannon 78
cacio e pepe 155, 165–6
cacio e pepe butter 32
Café de Paris butter 33
cakes 250
Breton cake 243
burnt butter sponge with burnt
buttercream 253–4
Christmas cake 350–1
dark chocolate and tahini babka 266–8
with fruit in 330
Hawaiian butter mochi cakes with
rosemary 204
quatre-quart cake 252
St Louis gooey butter cake 262
sticky gingerbread 194
Calvados: buckwheat galettes with butter-fried
apples and Calvados ice cream 337–8
capers: braised leeks with capers 122
caramel 190
salt and pepper caramels 208
salted caramel 207
cardamom: arlettes 310
date and cardamom butter 35
kardemummabullar 269–71
carrots: cumin, coriander and orange roasted
heritage carrots 117
champ 78
chaussons aux pommes 334–6
Cheddar: cheese twists 308
ploughman's quiche 228
Welsh rarebit gougères 257–8
cheese: cacio e pepe 165–6
cheese twists 308
griddled lettuce wedges with blue cheese
and walnut butter 124
Gruyère and spring onion soufflé 60–1

hasselbacks with kimchi and blue cheese
butter 74
Monte Cristo 180
Parmesan and black pepper sablés 240
ploughman's quiche 228
potted 153
tartiflette galette 244–5
Welsh rarebit gougères 257–8
cherries: boozy black cherry frangipane tart
232–4
ginger and sour cherry fudge 210–11
chicken: buffalo chicken wings 102
buttermilk fried chicken 184
chicken Kiev 99
chicken liver pâté 100
chicken skin butter 30
roast chicken 92
chillies: chipotle and coriander butter 93
jalapeño cornbread with honey butter 177
Turkish eggs with yoghurt and chilli
butter 54
chipotle and coriander butter 93
chives: sour cream and chive butter American
biscuits 289–90
chocolate: brown butter, milk chocolate and
pretzel blondies 198
brownies 196–7
dark chocolate and tahini babka 266–8
Earl Grey chocolate tart with chocolate
pastry 235–7
marmalade and dark chocolate bread and
butter pudding 344
Mars Bar Krispie bites 191
pains au chocolat 316
salted chocolate, hazelnut and rye
cookies 192–3
choux pastry 250–1
dauphine potatoes 81
Paris-Brest with praline mousseline 260–1
Welsh rarebit gougères 257–8
Christmas cake 350–1
Christmas pudding 352–3
fried in butter 357
cinnamon: arlettes 310

brown butter cinnamon rolls 264–5
clarified butter 40–3
clementine Sussex pond pudding 345–6
coconut: Anzac flapjacks 203
piña colada galette des rois 298–9
coconut milk: Hawaiian butter mochi cakes
with rosemary 204
cod: roasted cod with beurre blanc 141
colcannon 78
compound butters 19, 26–35, 93
condensed milk: ginger and sour cherry
fudge 210–11
Russian buttercream 217
cookies: salted chocolate, hazelnut and rye
cookies 192–3
see also biscuits
coriander: chipotle and coriander butter 93
coriander seeds: cumin, coriander and orange
roasted heritage carrots 117
orange and coriander seed palmiers 309
cornmeal: buttered polenta 174
jalapeño cornbread with honey butter 177
shrimp and grits 148
Coronation mayonnaise 81
crab butter 35
craquelin 251
Paris-Brest with praline mousseline 260–1
cream 106
cultured butter 24, 25
homemade butter 21
salt and pepper caramels 208
salted caramel 207
tartiflette galette 244–5
crème fraîche: cultured butter 24, 25
wild mushroom, tarragon and crème
fraîche pithivier 302–4
crème mousseline 219
Paris-Brest with praline mousseline 260–1
crème pâtissière: blackberry and bay custard
Danishes 318
pains au rhum et raisin 317
croissants 246, 313–15
crumble: damson plum crumble 349
crumpets 45

cultured butter 18, 24–5
    and vanilla shortbread 226
cumin, coriander and orange roasted heritage
    carrots 117
curd 48–9, 62
    passionfruit curd 62
    Seville orange curd 62
custard: rhubarb and custard doughnuts 272–5

D

dairy industry 11, 13
dal makhani 127
damson plum crumble 349
Danishes: blackberry and bay custard Danishes
    318
dates: Christmas pudding 352–3
    date and cardamom butter 35
    sticky date and fig pudding 341–2
dauphine potatoes 81
dill, pink peppercorn and sea salt butter 31
dinner rolls 171–2
doughnuts: dauphine potatoes 81
    rhubarb and custard doughnuts 272–5
duchess potatoes 78

E

Earl Grey chocolate tart with chocolate pastry
    235–7
egg whites 14
    honey and hazelnut friands 256
    Italian buttercream 218
    Swiss meringue buttercream 216
eggs 14, 48–9
    béarnaise 59
    blackberry and bay custard Danishes 318
    Breton cake 243
    brioche 276–7
    brown butter-basted fried eggs 52
    buckwheat galettes with butter-fried apples
        and Calvados ice cream 337–8
    buttermilk pancakes 183
    crème mousseline 219

duchess potatoes 78
French buttercream 218
hollandaise 57–8
marmalade and dark chocolate bread and
    butter pudding 344
Monte Cristo 180
omelette 50
pains au rhum et raisin 317
ploughman's quiche 228
rhubarb and custard doughnuts 272–5
scrambled eggs 51
tarte au citron 230–1
Turkish eggs 54
Welsh rarebit gougères 257–8
emulsions 86–7
ermine buttercream 217
espagnole 65
espresso butter 35
Ethiopian spiced butter 42

F

fat-washing 278–81
fazzoletti: sage butter fazzoletti 162–4
fermented butter 43
figs: Christmas pudding 352–3
    sticky date and fig pudding 341–2
filo pastry: baklava 200–2
fish 133–51
flapjacks: Anzac flapjacks 203
flavoured butters 19, 26–35, 93
fondant potatoes 79
frangipane: boozy black cherry frangipane
    tart 232–4
    piña colada galette des rois 298–9
French buttercream 218
French onion soup 121
French salted butter biscuits 238
friands: honey and hazelnut friands 256
fruit 330–1
    see also individual fruits
fruit cake 350–1
fudge 190
    ginger and sour cherry fudge 210–11

G

galette: fruit galette 330
galette des rois 298–9
galettes with butter-fried apples and Calvados
    ice cream 337–8
garlic butter pull-apart dinner rolls 171–2
German buttercream 219
ghee 40–1
    paratha 286
ginger: ginger and sour cherry fudge 210–11
gingerbread 194
    orange and ginger butter 34
gougères: Welsh rarebit gougères 257–8
green beans amandine 128
grits: shrimp and grits 148
Gruyère: Gruyère and spring onion soufflé
    60–1
    Monte Cristo 180

H

ham: Monte Cristo 180
hasselbacks with kimchi and blue cheese butter
    74
Hawaiian butter mochi cakes with rosemary
    204
hazelnuts: honey and hazelnut friands 256
    Paris-Brest with praline mousseline 260–1
    salted chocolate, hazelnut and rye cookies
        192–3
herb butter 27
hollandaise 57–8, 65
honey: baklava 200–2
    honey and hazelnut friands 256
    jalapeño cornbread with honey butter 177
horseradish: grilled kippers with horseradish
    butter 138

I

ice cream: buckwheat galettes with butter-fried
    apples and Calvados ice cream 337–8
infused butter 35
inverse puff pastry 300–1

J

jalapeño cornbread with honey butter 177

K

kardemummabullar 269–71
kaya toast 178
kielbasa sausage: Louisiana seafood boil 150
kimchi: hasselbacks with kimchi and blue
    cheese butter 74
kippers: grilled kippers with horseradish butter
    138
kouign amann 320–2

L

lamb chops with chipotle and coriander butter
    93
Lancashire butter pie 82
leeks: braised leeks with capers 122
lemons: tarte au citron 230–1
lentils: dal makhani 127
lettuce: griddled lettuce wedges with blue
    cheese and walnut butter 124
liver: chicken liver pâté 100
lobster 134
    hot buttered lobster rolls 144–6
Louisiana seafood boil 150

M

Maltaise sauce 58
maple syrup: rosemary and maple syrup butter
    34
margarine 108–9
marmalade and dark chocolate bread and butter
    pudding 344
Marmite: Nigella's Marmite spaghetti 158
Marmite butter 32
    Marmite butter potatoes 73
Mars Bar Krispie bites 191
marshmallow crispy bites 39
mashed potatoes 76–8
mayonnaise: dauphine potatoes 81

meat 91–105
meringue: burnt butter sponge with burnt
    buttercream 253–4
    Italian buttercream 218
    Swiss meringue buttercream 216
milk: crème mousseline 219
    ermine buttercream 217
mille-feuille: blackberry and pistachio
    mille-feuille 305–6
miso butter roasted baby radishes 118
mochi: Hawaiian butter mochi cakes with
    rosemary 204
Monte Cristo 180
muffins 45
mushrooms: wild mushroom, tarragon and
    crème fraîche pithiver 302–4

N

niter kibbeh 42

O

oats: Anzac flapjacks 203
old fashioned: brown butter old fashioned 280
omelette 50
onions: French onion soup 121
    Lancashire butter pie 82
    slow-roasted muscovado onions 116
    see also pickled onions; spring onions
oranges: cumin, coriander and orange roasted
    heritage carrots 117
    grilled scallops with Seville orange and
      seaweed butter 136
    orange and coriander seed palmiers 309
    orange and ginger butter 34
    Seville orange curd 62
oven temperatures 14
oysters Rockefeller 147

P

pains au chocolat 316
pains au rhum et raisin 317
palmiers: orange and coriander seed palmiers

309
pancakes: buckwheat galettes with butter-fried
    apples and Calvados ice cream 337–8
    buttermilk pancakes 183
paratha 286
Paris-Brest with praline mousseline 260–1
Parmesan and black pepper sablés 240
passionfruit curd 62
pasta 155–6
    cacio e pepe 165–6
    Nigella's Marmite spaghetti 158
    sage butter fazzoletti 162–4
pastry 222–3, 246–7
    blackberry and bay custard Danishes 318
    boozy black cherry frangipane tart 232–4
    cheese twists 308
    croissants 313–15
    Earl Grey chocolate tart with chocolate
      pastry 235–7
    kouign amann 320–2
    pains au chocolat 316
    pains au rhum et raisin 317
    ploughman's quiche 228
    rye treacle tart 229
    tarte au citron 230–1
    see also choux pastry; puff pastry
pâté: chicken liver pâté 100
pâte sablée 222
pâte sucrée 222
peas: risi e bisi 170
pecans: baklava 200–2
    brown butter bourbon pecan sandies 281
pecorino: cacio e pepe 165–6
pepper: cacio e pepe 165–6
    Parmesan and black pepper sablés 240
    salt and pepper caramels 208
pickled onions: ploughman's quiche 228
pilaf: buttery pilaf 159
piña colada galette des rois 298–9
pineapple: Christmas cake 350–1
    piña colada galette des rois 298–9
    pineapple upside down tarte Tatin 343
pink peppercorns: dill, pink peppercorn and sea
    salt butter 31

pistachios: baklava 200–2
    blackberry and pistachio mille-feuille
        305–6
pithivier: wild mushroom, tarragon and crème
    fraîche pithiver 302–4
ploughman's quiche 228
plums: damson plum crumble 349
polenta: buttered polenta 174
pork: butter-basted pork chops 96–8
potatoes 68
    baked potato 70
    dauphine potatoes 81
    fondant potatoes 79
    hasselbacks with kimchi and blue cheese
        butter 74
    Lancashire butter pie 82
    Marmite butter potatoes 73
    mashed potatoes 76–8
    potato pavé 84
    potato rösti 69
    tartiflette galette 244–5
potting 152–3
prawns: Louisiana seafood boil 150
pretzels: brown butter, milk chocolate and
    pretzel blondies 198
prunes: Christmas pudding 352–3
puff pastry 246, 284–5, 296–7
    apple turnovers 334–6
    arlettes 310
    blackberry and pistachio mille-feuille
        305–6
    fruit galette 330
    inverse puff pastry 300–1
    orange and coriander seed palmiers 309
    piña colada galette des rois 298–9
    using scraps 308–10
    wild mushroom, tarragon and crème
        fraîche pithiver 302–4
    see also rough puff pastry

Q

quiche: ploughman's quiche 228
quince turnovers 336

R

rabbit: potted 153
radishes: miso butter roasted baby radishes 118
raisins: pains au rhum et raisin 317
Reblochon: tartiflette galette 244–5
rhubarb: rhubarb and custard doughnuts 272–5
    rhubarb turnovers 336
rice 155
    buttery pilaf 159
    risi e bisi 170
    risotto Milanese 169
    saffron and yoghurt tahdig 160
rice flour: Hawaiian butter mochi cakes with
    rosemary 204
Rice Krispies: Mars Bar Krispie bites 191
    marshmallow crispy bites 39
risi e bisi 170
risotto Milanese 169
rosemary: Hawaiian butter mochi cakes with
    rosemary 204
    rosemary and maple syrup butter 34
rösti 69
rough puff pastry 291
    rough puff sausage rolls 294
rum: bananas Foster 332
    pains au rhum et raisin 317
Russian buttercream 217
rye flour: salted chocolate, hazelnut and rye
    cookies 192–3
rye treacle tart 229

S

sablé Breton 222
    French salted butter biscuits 238
sablés: Parmesan and black pepper sablés 240
saffron: saffron buns 263
    saffron and yoghurt tahdig 160
sage butter fazzoletti 162–4
St Louis gooey butter cake 262
salt 10–11, 20–1, 107
    dill, pink peppercorn and sea salt butter 31
    salt and pepper caramels 208
    salted caramel 207

salted chocolate, hazelnut and rye cookies
    192–3
sandies: brown butter bourbon pecan sandies
    281
sandwiches 44
    Monte Cristo 180
    Singaporean kaya toast 178
sauces 64–5
    béarnaise 59
    beurre blanc 141
    emulsions 86–7
    hollandaise 59
sausages: Louisiana seafood boil 150
    sausage rolls 294
scallops: grilled scallops with Seville orange and
    seaweed butter 136
schnitzel 104
scones 224
scrambled eggs 51
sculpture 130–1
seafood boil 150
seaweed butter 31
    grilled scallops with Seville orange and
        seaweed butter 136
Seville oranges: grilled scallops with Seville
    orange and seaweed butter 136
    marmalade and dark chocolate bread and
        butter pudding 344
    Seville orange curd 62
shallots: slow-roasted muscovado onions 116
    tartiflette galette 244–5
shortbread: vanilla shortbread 226
shortcrust pastry 246
shrimp: potted 152–3
    shrimp and grits 148
Singaporean kaya toast 178
smen 43
smoked butter 22
soda bread 186
sole meunière 142
soufflés 49
    Gruyère and spring onion soufflé 60–1
soup 45
    French onion soup 121

BUTTER – A CELEBRATION

sour cream and chive butter American biscuits 289–90

spaghetti: Marmite spaghetti 158

spring onions: champ 78

    Gruyère and spring onion soufflé 60–1

state fairs 130–1

steamed puddings 331

    Christmas pudding 352–3

    Christmas pudding fried in butter 357

    sticky date and fig pudding 341–2

sticky date and fig pudding 341–2

Stilton: hasselbacks with kimchi and blue cheese butter 74

suet: clementine Sussex pond pudding 345–6

sugar 189–219

sultanas: pains au rhum et raisin 317

Sussex pond pudding 345–6

sweetcorn: jalapeño cornbread with honey butter 177

    Louisiana seafood boil 150

Swiss meringue buttercream 216

    burnt butter sponge with burnt buttercream 253–4

T

tahdig 160

tahini: dark chocolate and tahini babka 266–8

tarragon: béarnaise 59

    wild mushroom, tarragon and crème fraîche pithiver 302–4

tarte au citron 230–1

tarte Tatin 343

tartiflette galette 244–5

toast 44–5

    Singaporean kaya toast 178

toffee 190

    almond butter toffee brittle 212

treacle soda bread 186

treacle tart 229

trout: with buttered almonds 135

turkey: butter shroud turkey 94

Turkish eggs 54

U

Ukrainian burnt aubergine butter 129

urad dal: dal makhani 127

V

vanilla: vanilla shortbread 226

veal: Wiener schnitzel 104

vegetables 112–13

    see also individual vegetables

velouté 65

W

waffles: buttermilk waffles 183

walnuts: baklava 200–2

    griddled lettuce wedges with blue cheese and walnut butter 124

Welsh rarebit gougères 257–8

Wiener schnitzel 104

Wild garlic butter 27

wine: tartiflette galette 244–5

Y

yeast 15

yoghurt: saffron and yoghurt tahdig 160

    Turkish eggs with yoghurt and chilli butter 54

Conversion charts

Weight conversions

25/30g	1oz
40g	1½oz
50g	1¾oz
55g	2oz
70g	2½oz
85g	3oz
100g	3½oz
115g	4oz
150g	5½oz
200g	7oz
225g	8oz
250g	9oz
300g	10½oz
350g	12oz
375g	13oz
400g	14oz
450g	1lb
500g	1lb 2oz
600g	1lb 5oz
750g	1lb 10oz
900g	2lb
1kg	2lb 4oz
2kg	4lb 8oz

Length

1cm	½ inch
2.5cm	1 inch
3cm	1¼ inches
5cm	2 inches
8cm	3¼ inches
10cm	4 inches
20cm	8 inches
25cm	10 inches

Volume conversions (liquids)

5ml	—	1 tsp
15ml	½fl oz	1 tbsp
30ml	1fl oz	2 tbsp
60ml	2fl oz	¼ cup
75ml	2½fl oz	⅓ cup
120ml	4fl oz	½ cup
150ml	5fl oz	⅔ cup
175ml	6fl oz	¾ cup
250ml	8fl oz	1 cup
350ml	12fl oz	1½ cups
500ml	18fl oz	2 cups
1 litre	1¾ pints	4 cups

Volume conversions
(dry ingredients – an approximate guide)

Flour	125g	1 cup
Butter	225g	1 cup (2 sticks)
Breadcrumbs (dried)	125g	1 cup
Nuts	125g	1 cup
Seeds	160g	1 cup
Dried fruit	150g	1 cup
Dried pulses (large)	175g	1 cup
Grains & small pulses	200g	1 cup

Oven temperatures

°C	°C with fan	°F	gas mark
110°C	90°C	225°	F ¼
120°C	100°C	250°	F ½
140°C	120°C	275°	F 1
150°C	130°C	300°	F 2
160°C	140°C	325°	F 3
180°C	160°C	350°	F 4
190°C	170°C	375°	F 5
200°C	180°C	400°	F 6
220°C	200°C	425°	F 7
230°C	210°C	450°	F 8
240°C	220°C	475°	F 9